Dinosaur Therapy

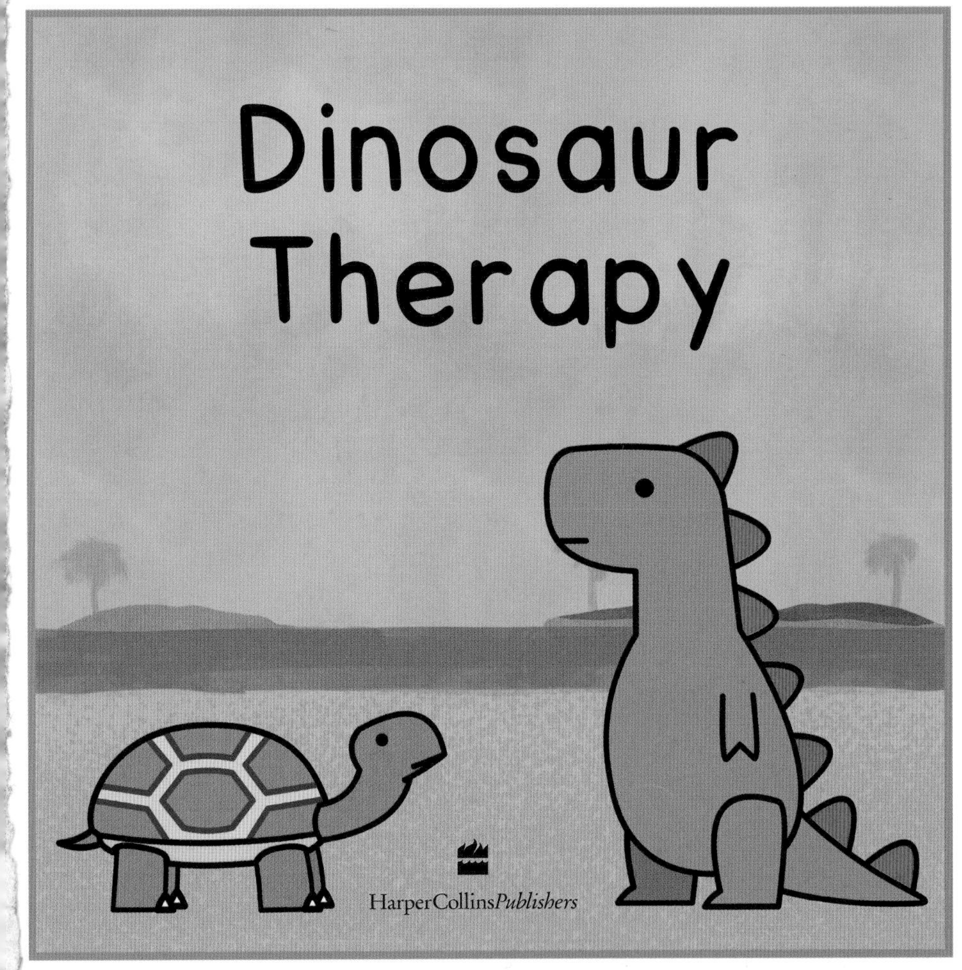

HarperCollins*Publishers*

HarperCollins*Publishers*
1 London Bridge Street
London SE1 9GF

www.harpercollins.co.uk

HarperCollins*Publishers*
Macken House, 39/40 Mayor Street Upper, Dublin 1, D01 C9W8, Ireland

First published by HarperCollins*Publishers* 2021

12

Text © James Stewart 2021
Illustrations © K Roméy 2021

Hey Buddy Comics assert the moral right to be
identified as the authors of this work

A catalogue record of this book is
available from the British Library

ISBN 978-0-00-847281-8

Printed and bound in Latvia

MIX
Paper | Supporting
responsible forestry
FSC
www.fsc.org
FSC™ C007454

This book is produced from
independently certified FSC™ paper
to ensure responsible forest management.
For more information visit: www.harpercollins.co.uk/green

Contents

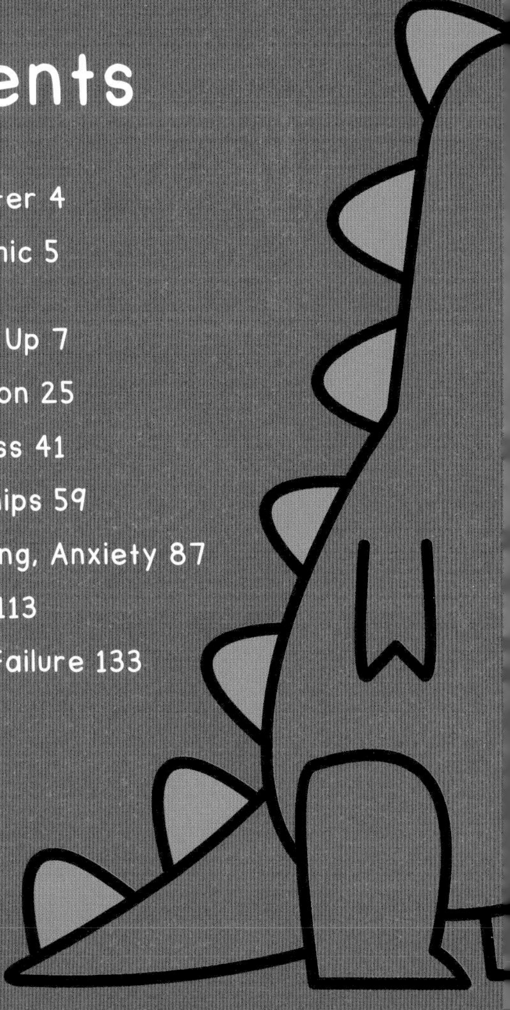

The Writer

I was diagnosed with ADHD in 2019, and by the end of 2020 I had turned writing webcomics into my full-time job. The path between these two was not a straight one, but what the diagnosis did give me was excuses; excuses in the best possible sense.

First, I no longer had to wonder why I was not only miserable working in an office, but also uniquely bad at it. Wishing to escape the 9-to-5 grind was no longer a selfish fantasy, but a self-preservation necessity.

Second, I no longer saw my depression as a general malaise preventing me from doing things and stepping outside my comfort zone. I now had a specific excuse: my ADHD made it difficult for me to work in the normal way, and to feel better I had to find a different way to do things.

Third, my inability to focus on writing long enough to say the things I wanted to say was no longer a reflection on my writing ability. I could write fine - I just had to find the right medium to quickly and clearly capture my thoughts before my mind moved on to something else.

Enter K, my friend, artist and collaborator, and the beginning of Dinos and Comics.

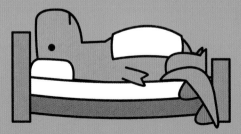

The Comic

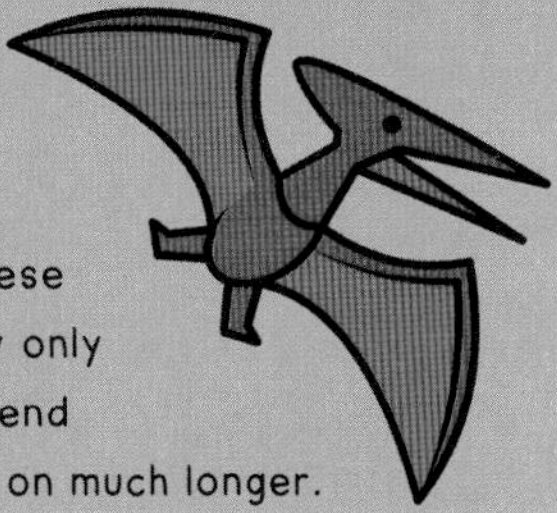

One question you might expect an introduction like this to answer is: why dinosaurs? I'd love to have some fancy answer about how abstracting away from our particular species both physically and temporally helps me reveal deeper truths about the human condition. But the honest answer is that we picked dinosaurs because they are cool and K was pretty good at drawing them. Maybe there's something in the former thought, but if there is, it's merely a happy accident.

I've no doubt that one of the reasons the comic connected with people so quickly is timing. It launched in September 2020 when the Covid-19 pandemic had become a normal part of life and there was no end in sight. Not only were people locked in their houses looking for new things to entertain them, but loneliness, depression and anxiety were all on the rise, and the comic spoke to these issues in a way people could relate to. But while the pandemic has caused a spike in these issues, it is in reality only a quickening of a trend that has been going on much longer. Every year more people live their lives with some kind of mental health issue hanging over them. I hope that talking about mental health in a blunt and open way offers some people some catharsis, however brief.

While a lot of the comic strips do focus on the struggles of living with mental health issues, I also want them to be hopeful. That's why there's a focus on relationships, because in an increasingly atomised world only our connections with other people can save us. It's also why I repeatedly try to highlight the way modern working conditions – and the impermanent and contingent nature of the way we live – affect our mental health. Yes, we live in a society, but to paraphrase David Graeber, we also built that society and we could just as easily build a new one.

growing up

learning things i did not want to know

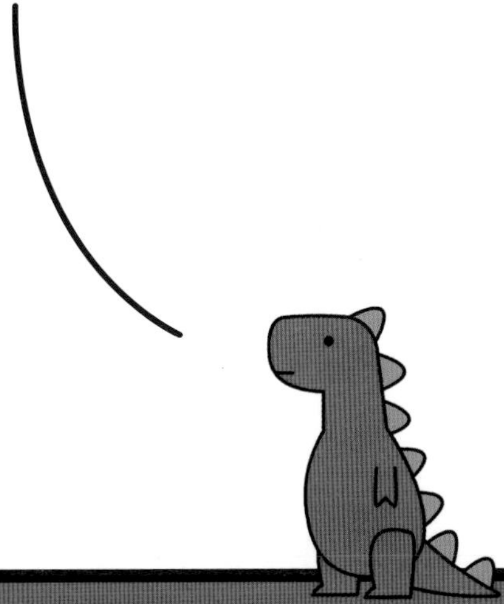

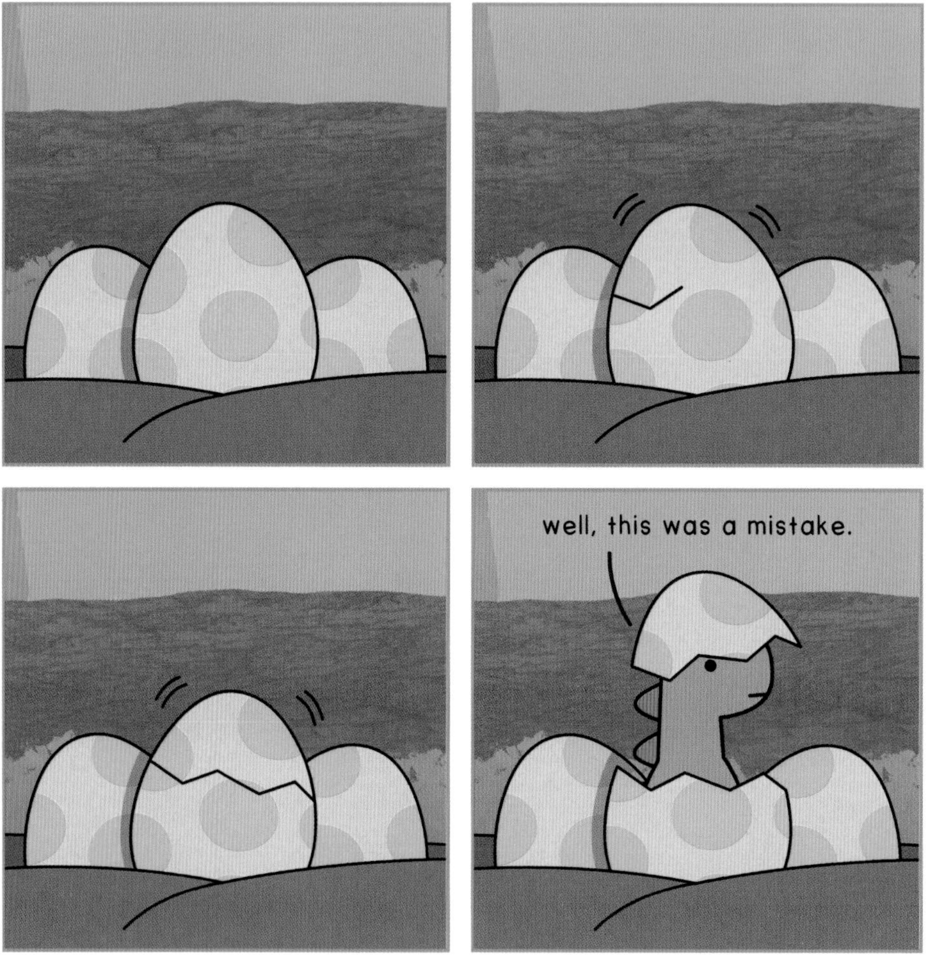
well, this was a mistake.

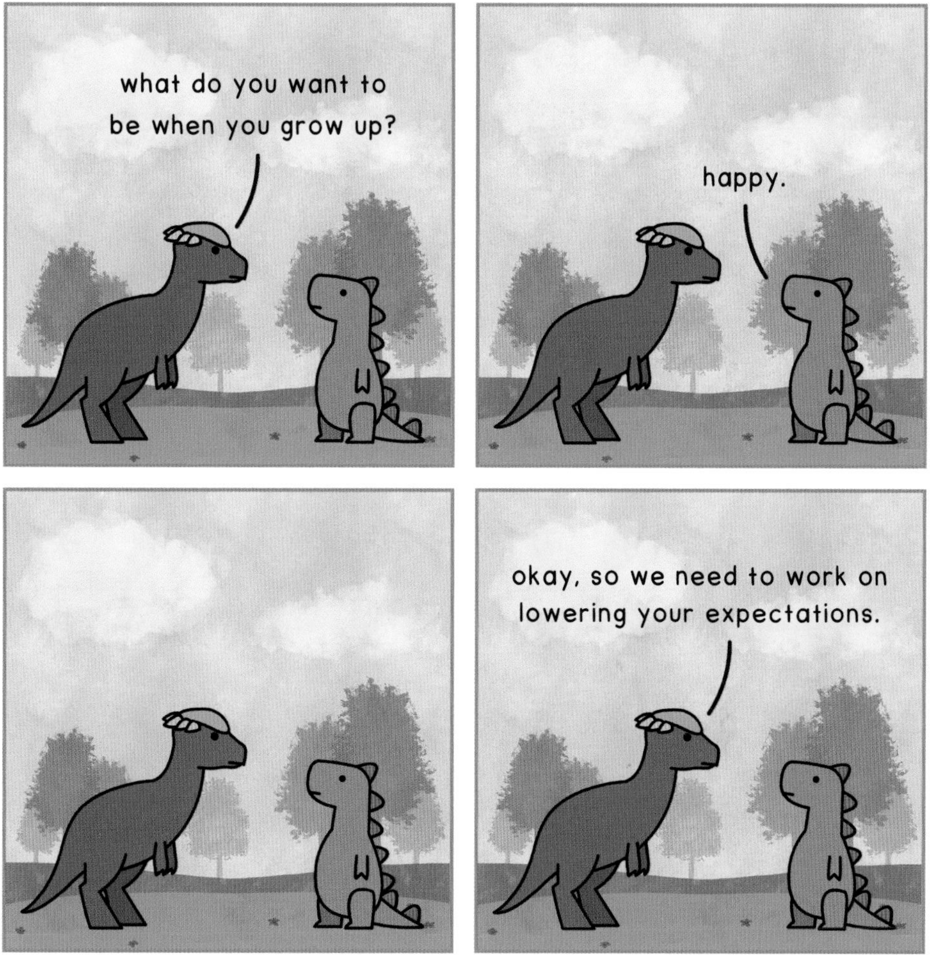
what do you want to be when you grow up?
happy.
okay, so we need to work on lowering your expectations.

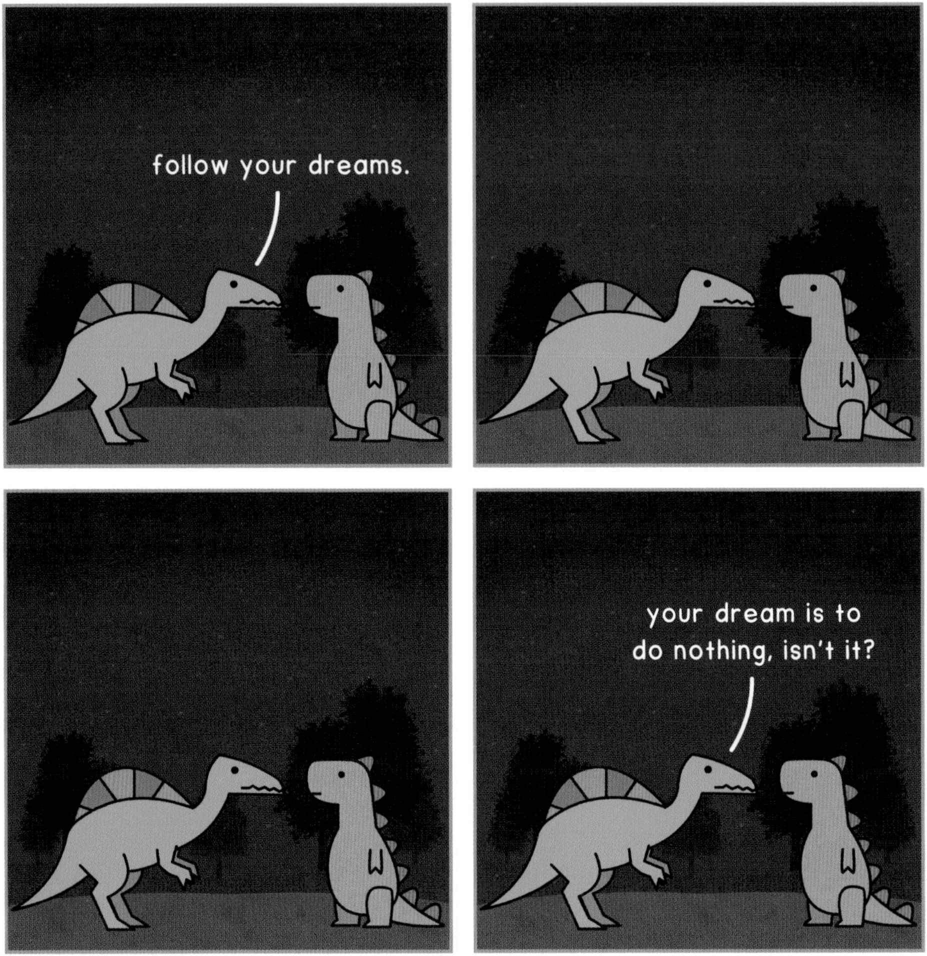
follow your dreams.
your dream is to do nothing, isn't it?

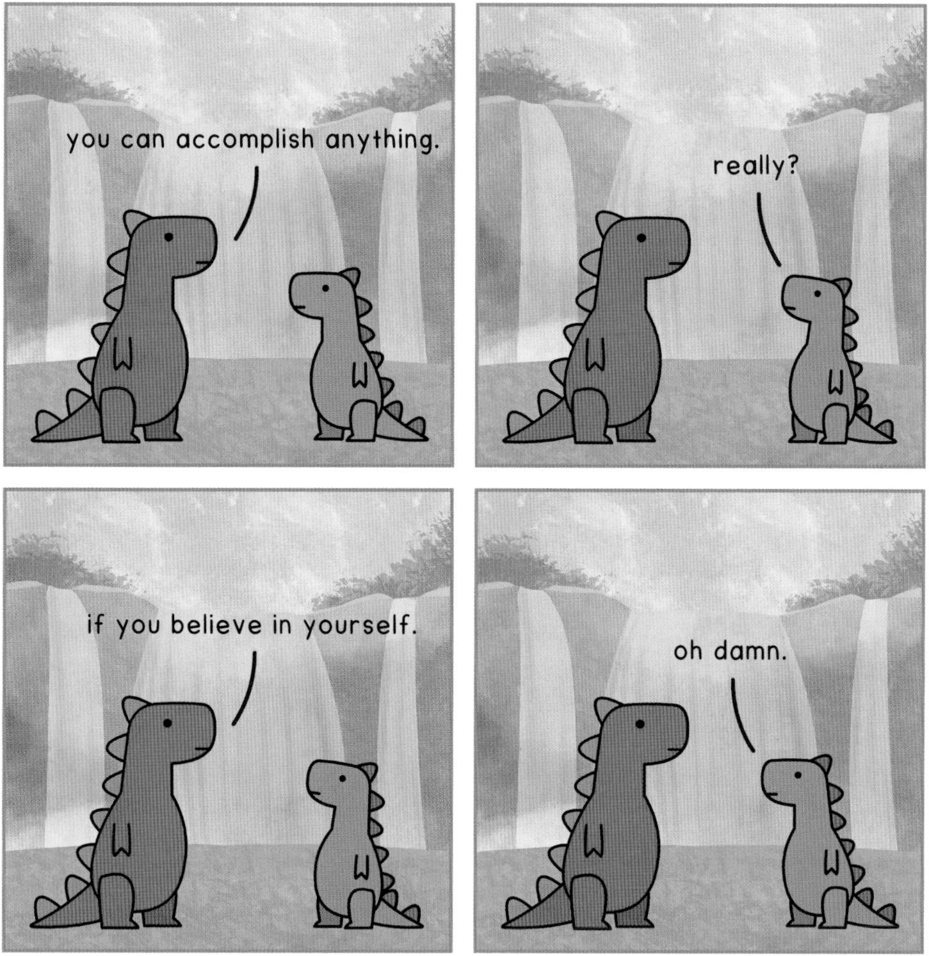
you can accomplish anything.
really?
if you believe in yourself.
oh damn.

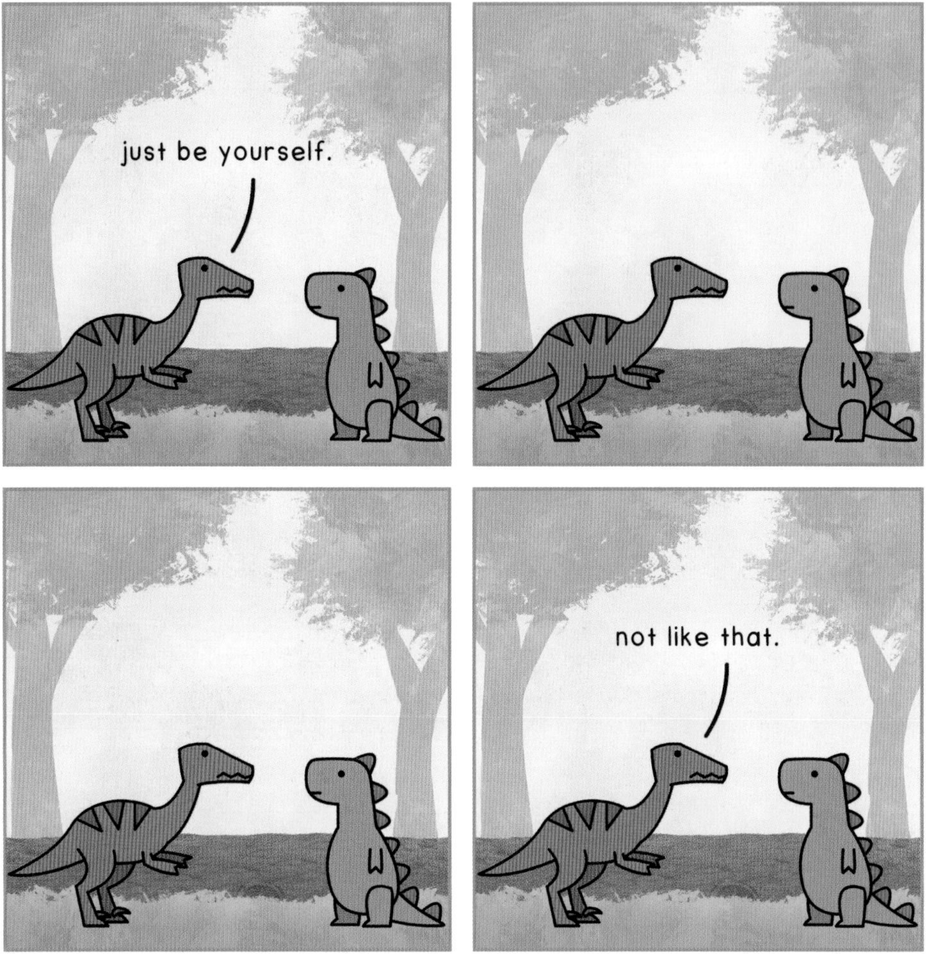
just be yourself.
not like that.

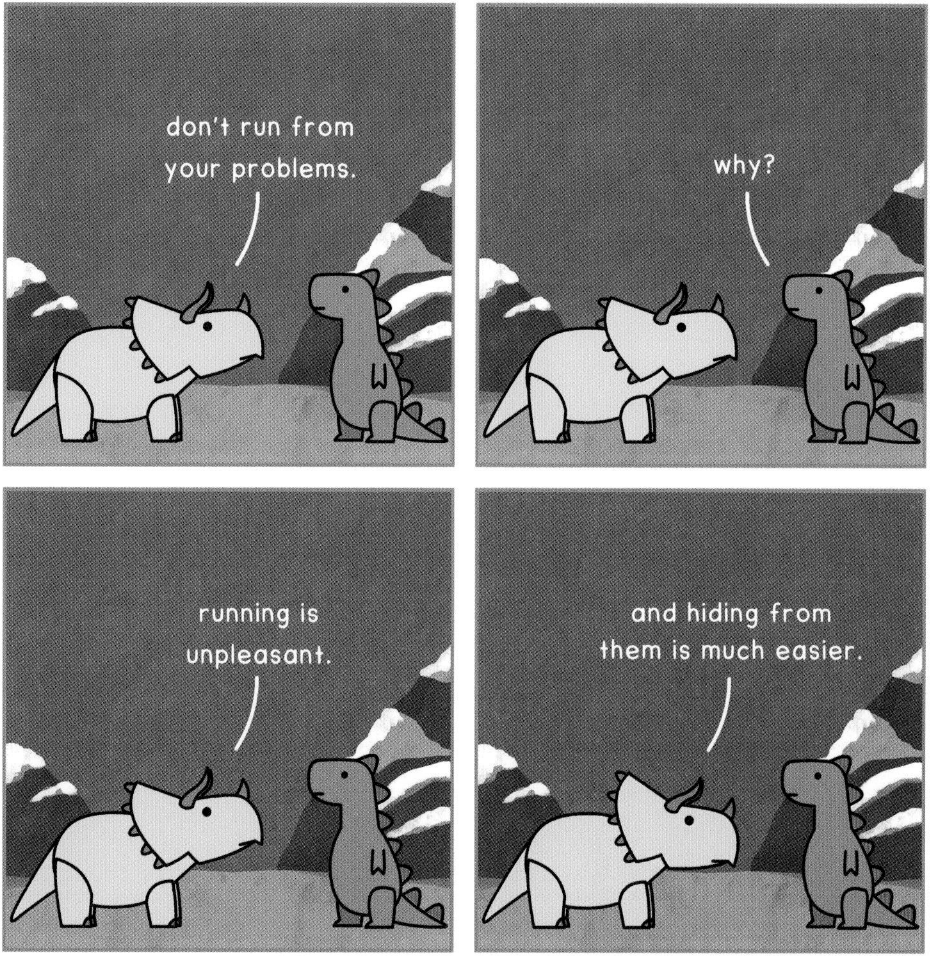
don't run from your problems.
why?
running is unpleasant.
and hiding from them is much easier.

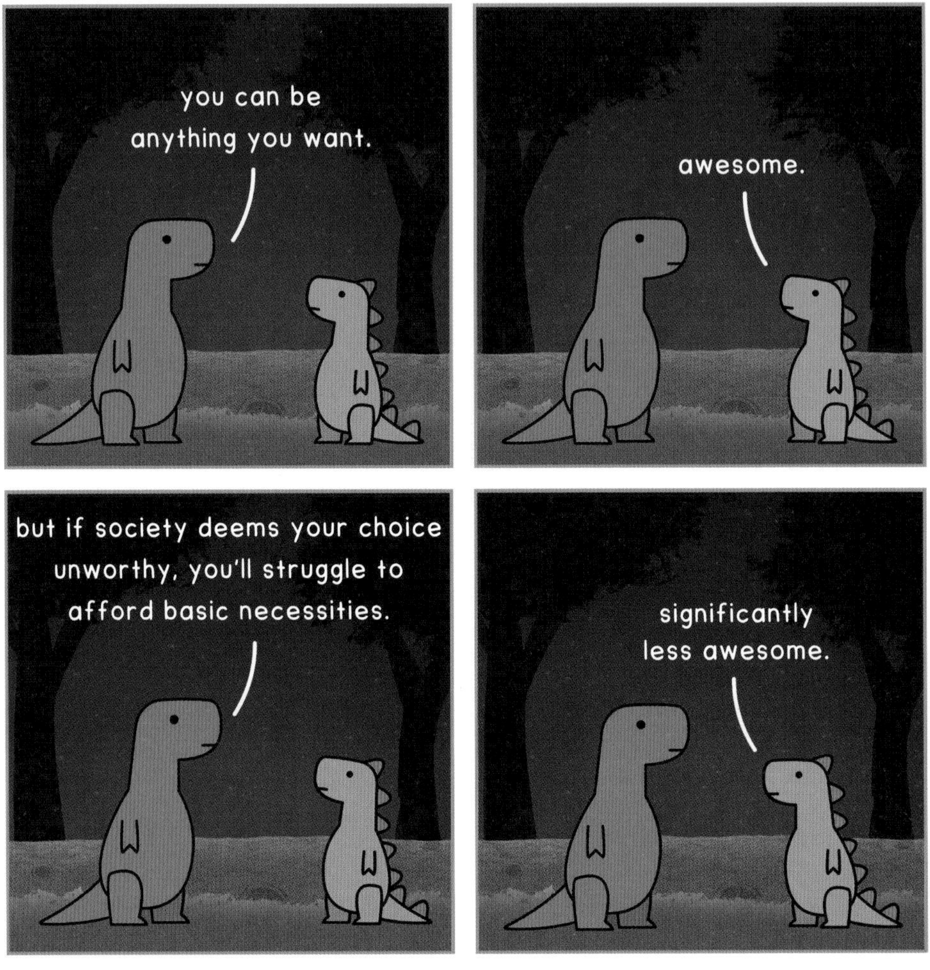
you can be anything you want.
awesome.
but if society deems your choice unworthy, you'll struggle to afford basic necessities.
significantly less awesome.

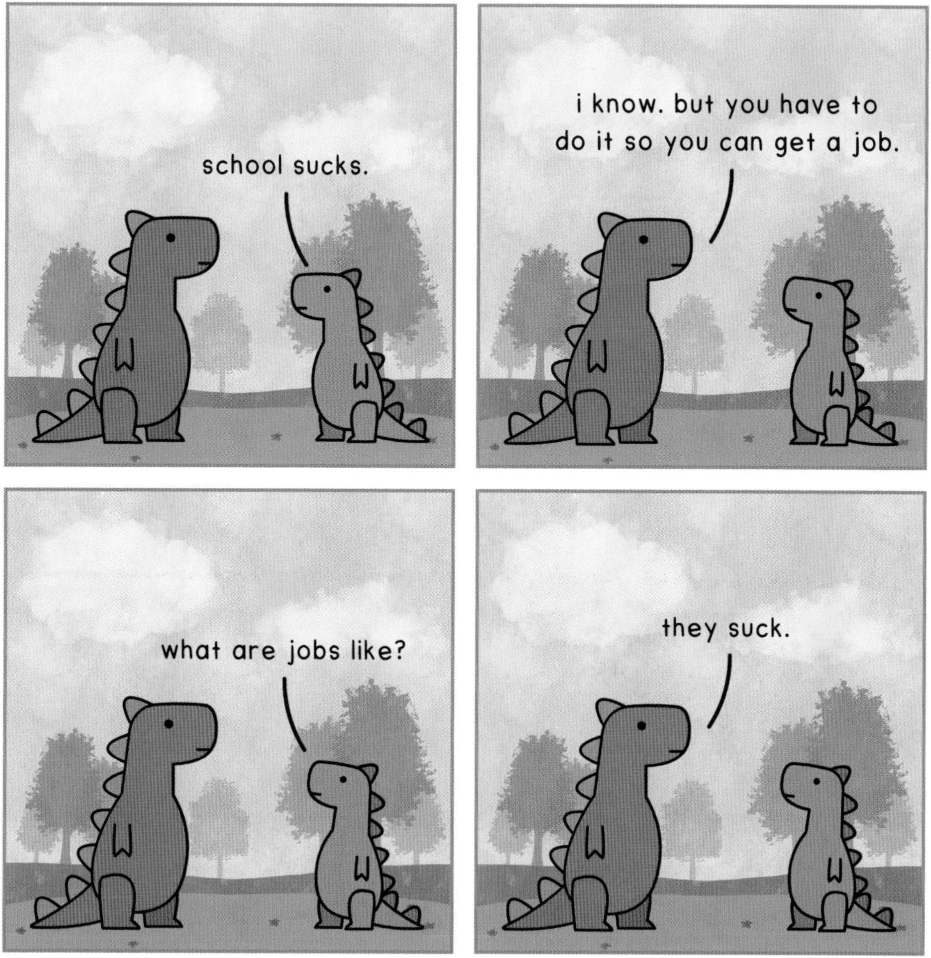
school sucks.
i know. but you have to do it so you can get a job.
what are jobs like?
they suck.

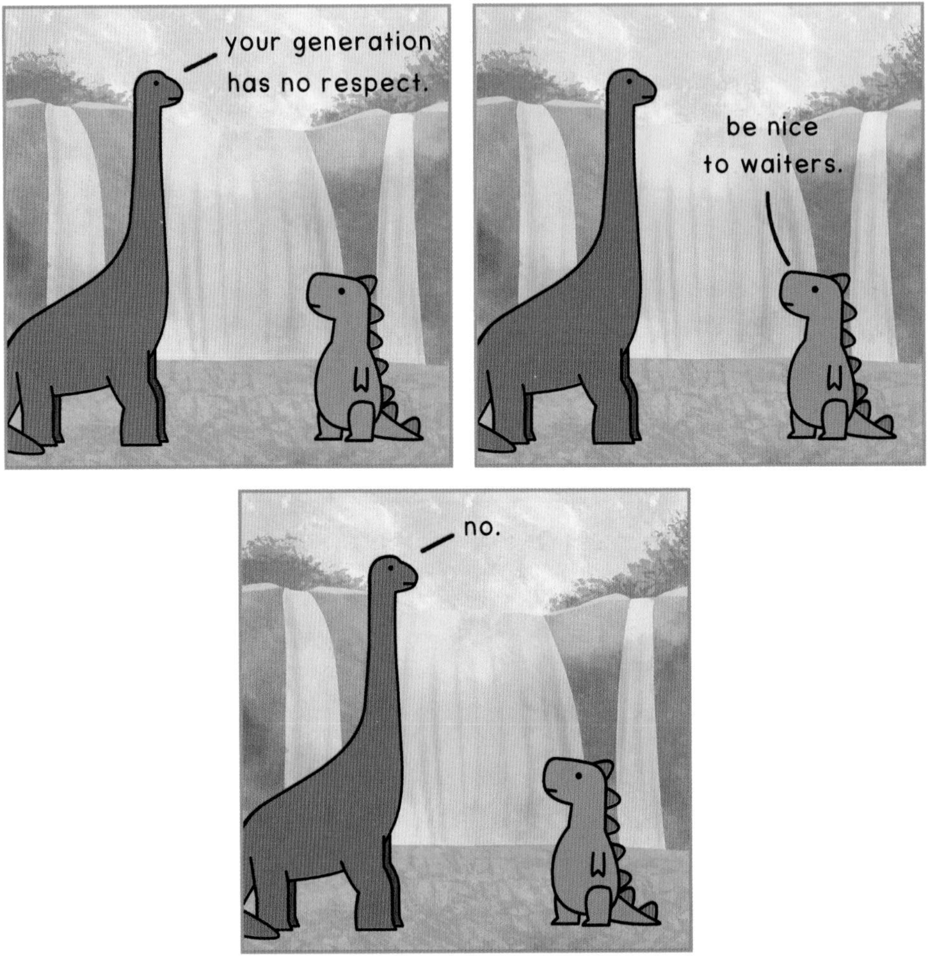
your generation has no respect.
be nice to waiters.
no.

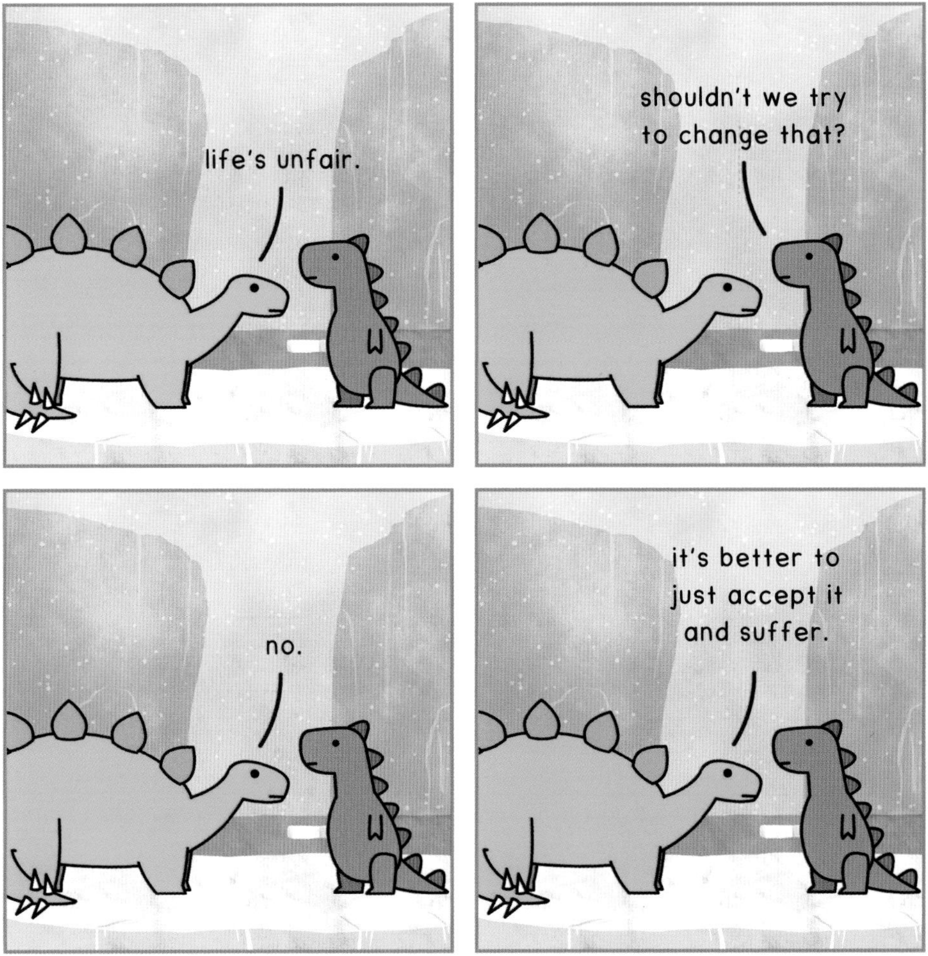
life's unfair.
shouldn't we try to change that?
no.
it's better to just accept it and suffer.

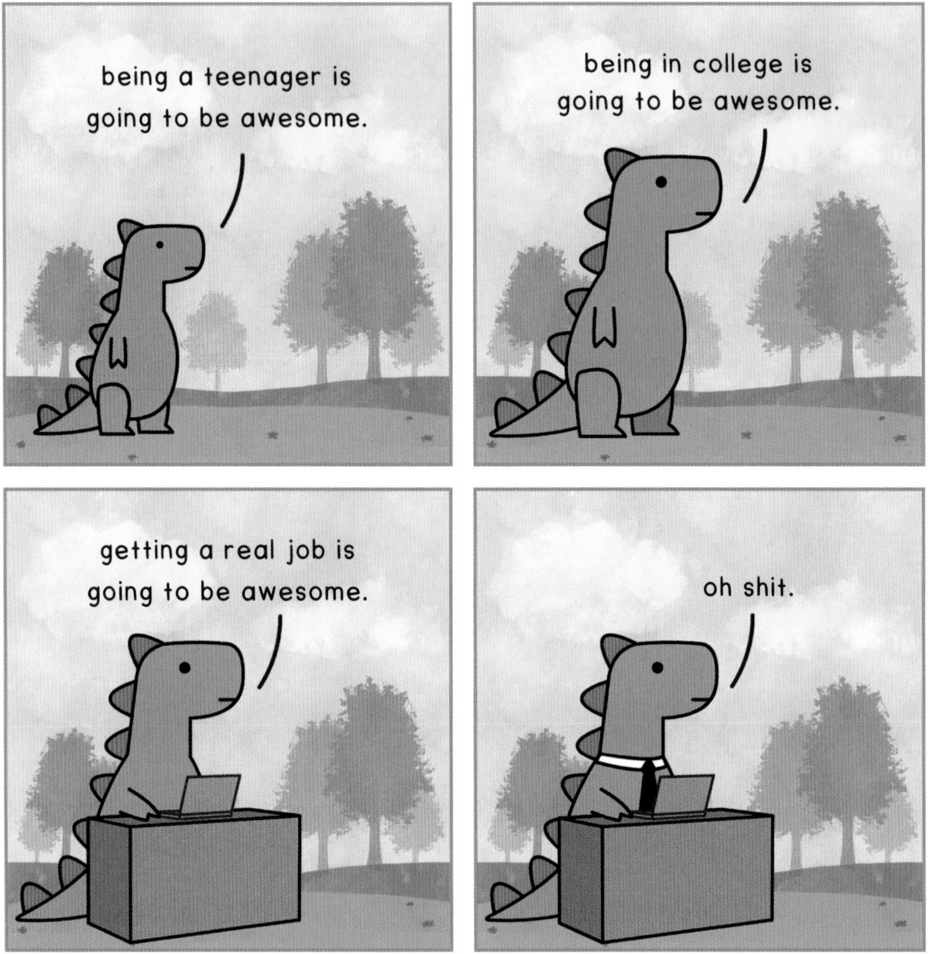
being a teenager is
going to be awesome.
being in college is
going to be awesome.
getting a real job is
going to be awesome.
oh shit.

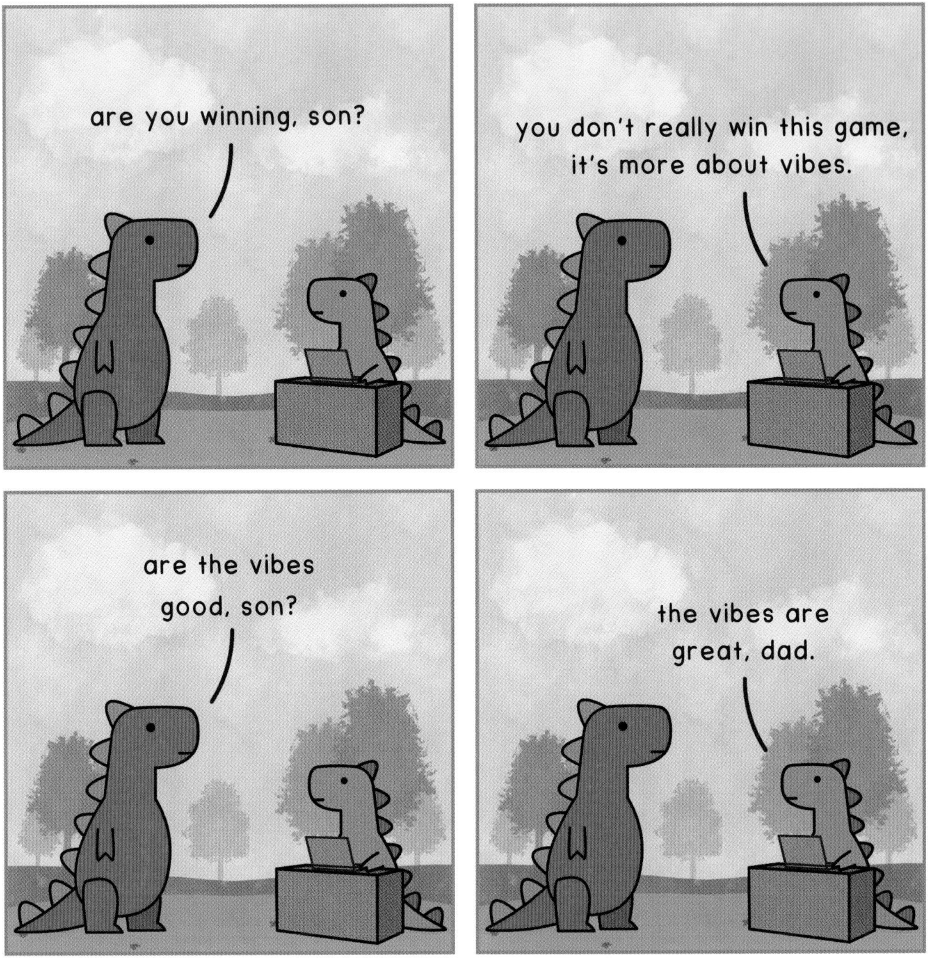
are you winning, son?
you don't really win this game, it's more about vibes.
are the vibes good, son?
the vibes are great, dad.

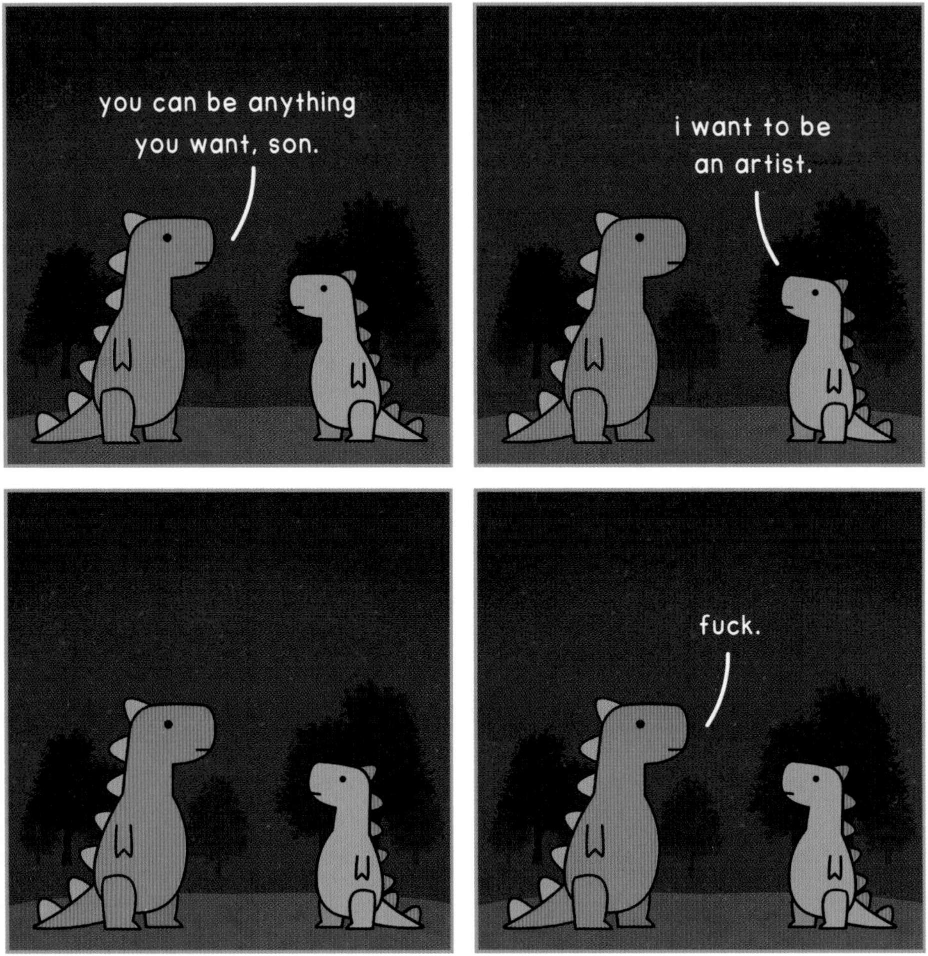
you can be anything
you want, son.
i want to be
an artist.
fuck.

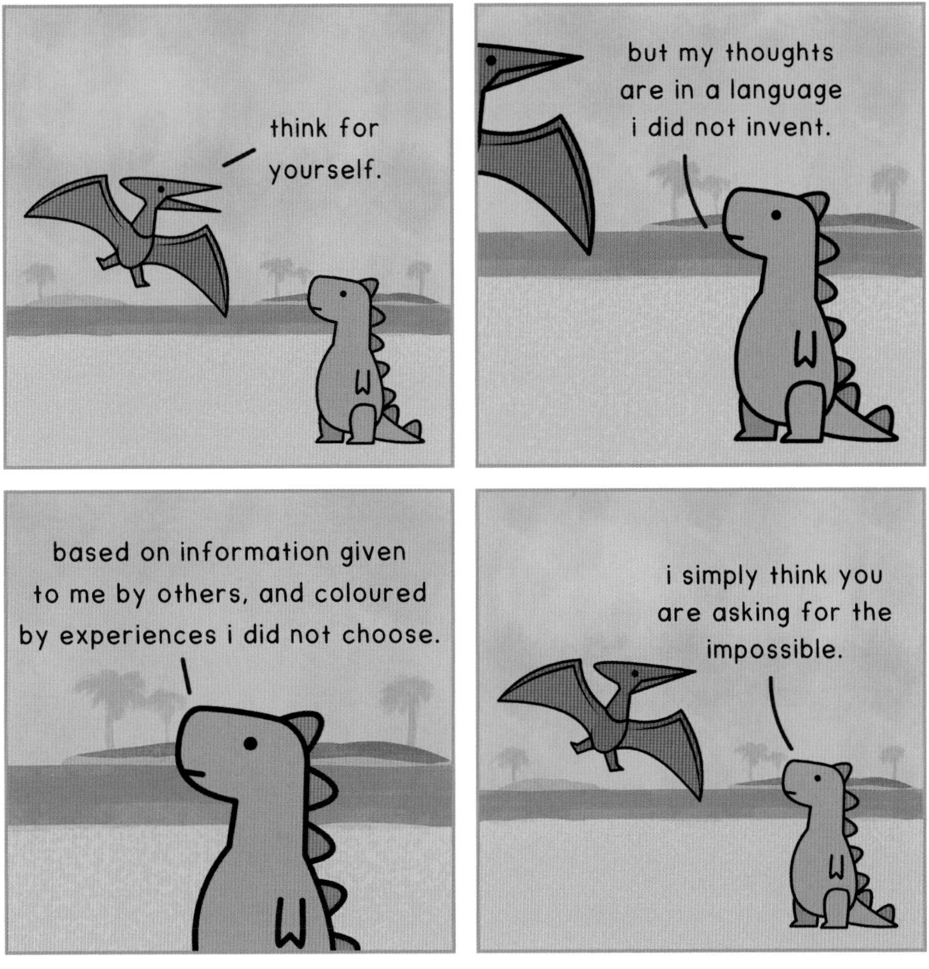
think for yourself.
but my thoughts are in a language i did not invent.
based on information given to me by others, and coloured by experiences i did not choose.
i simply think you are asking for the impossible.

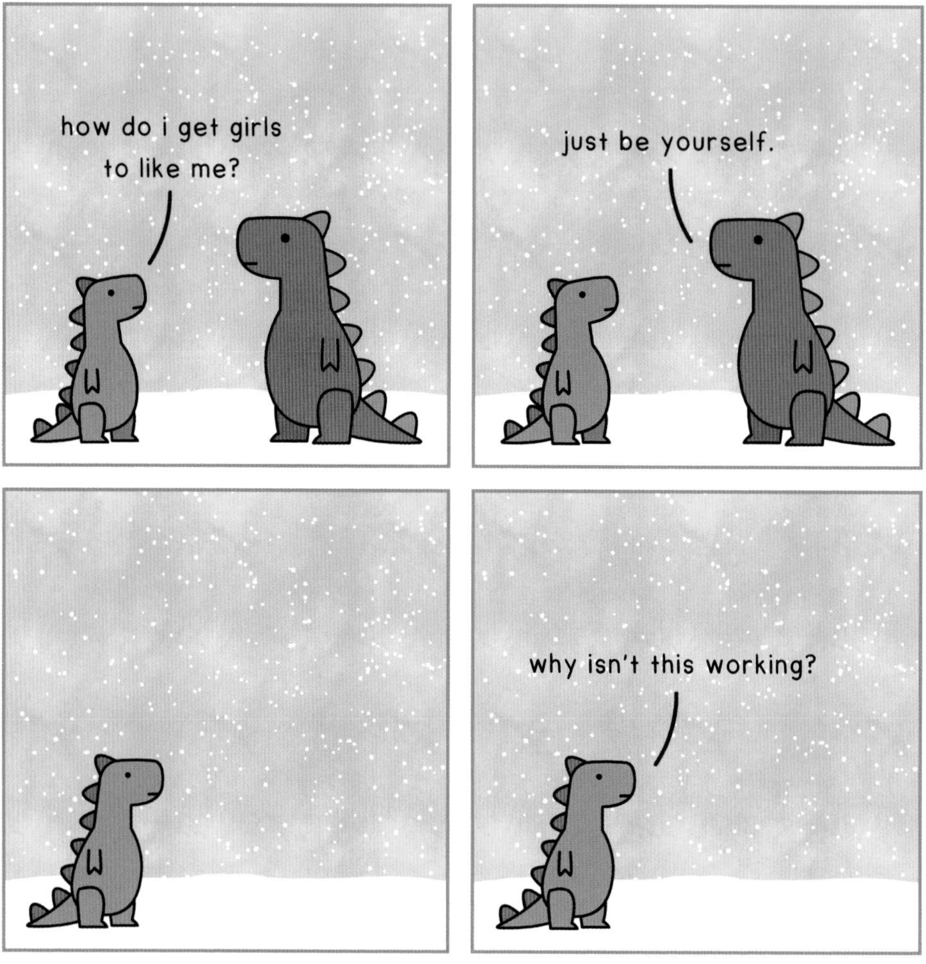
how do i get girls to like me?
just be yourself.
why isn't this working?

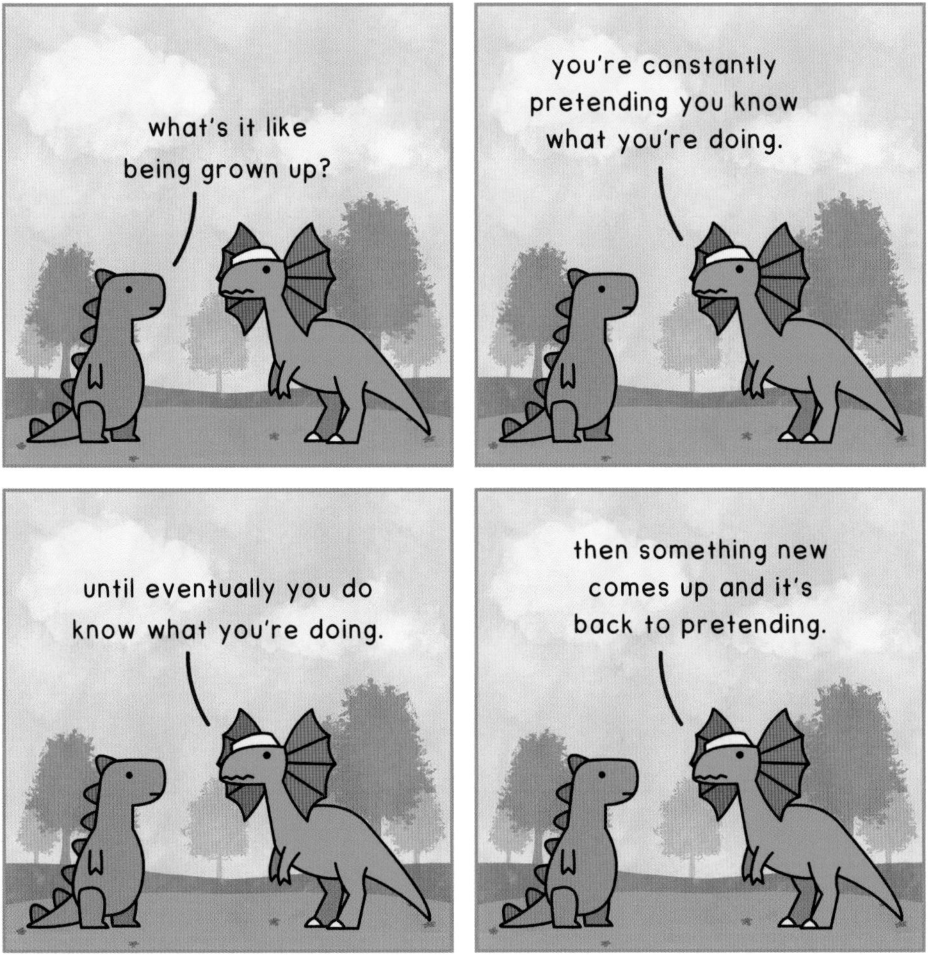
what's it like
being grown up?
you're constantly
pretending you know
what you're doing.
until eventually you do
know what you're doing.
then something new
comes up and it's
back to pretending.

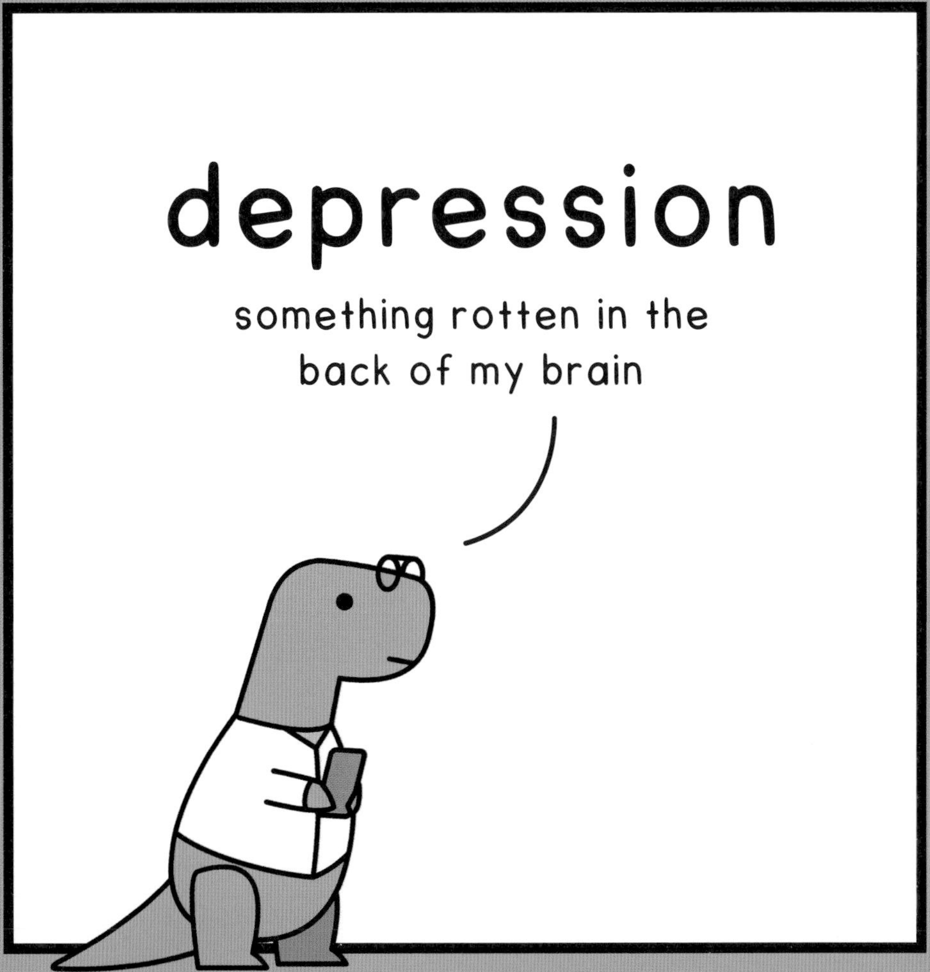
depression
something rotten in the back of my brain

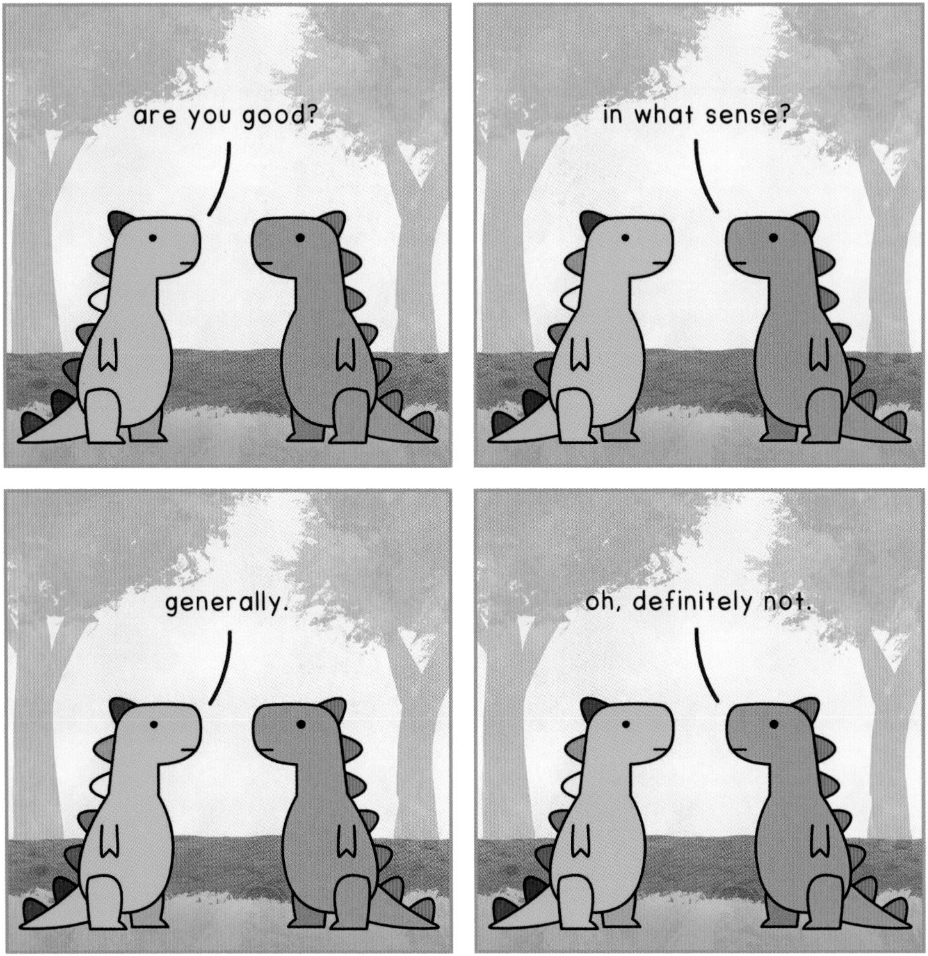
are you good?
in what sense?
generally.
oh, definitely not.

everybody hates you.
anxiety
for good reason.
depression

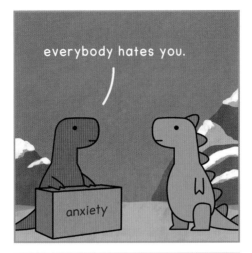

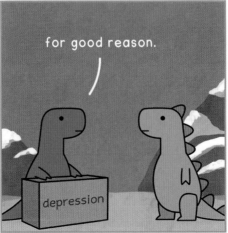

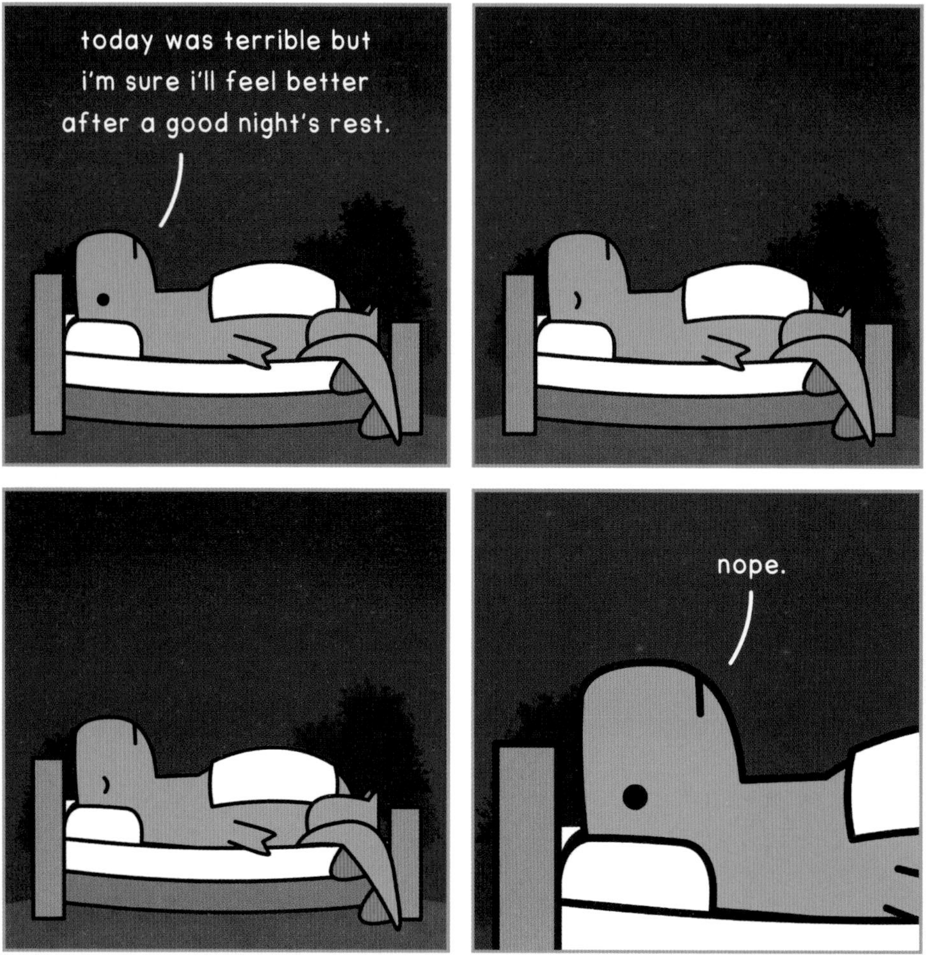
today was terrible but i'm sure i'll feel better after a good night's rest.
nope.

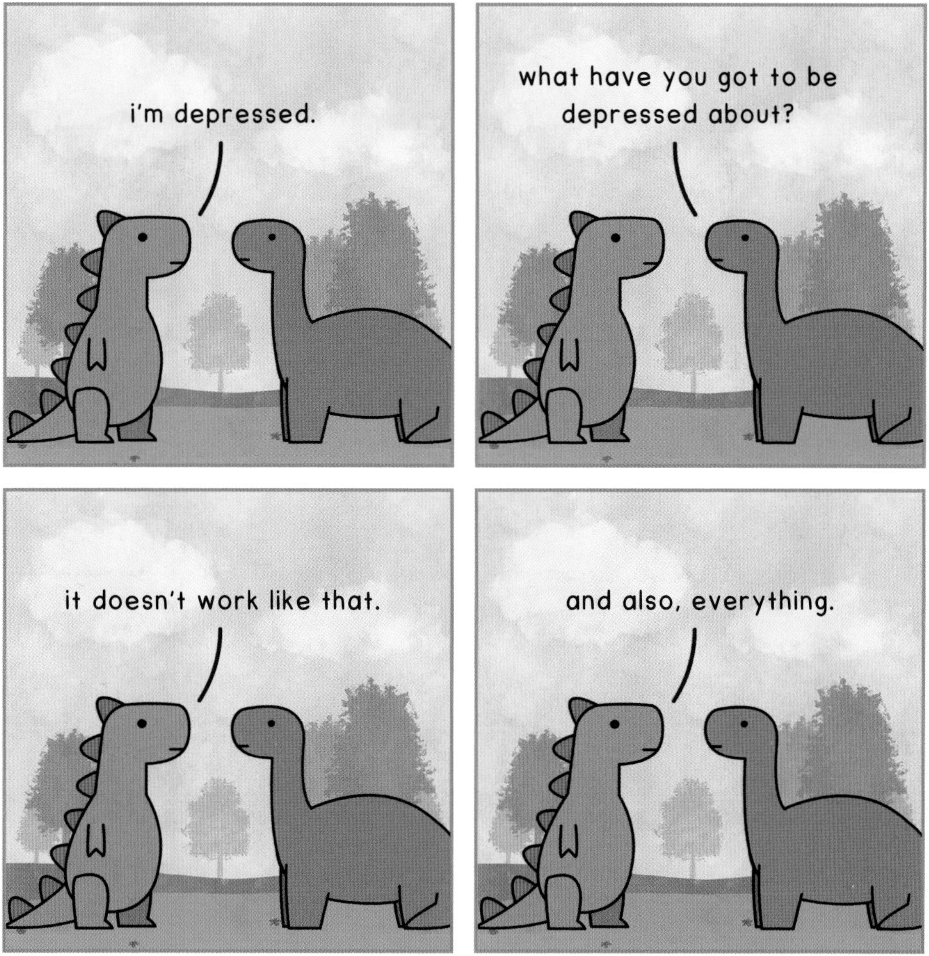
i'm depressed.
what have you got to be depressed about?
it doesn't work like that.
and also, everything.

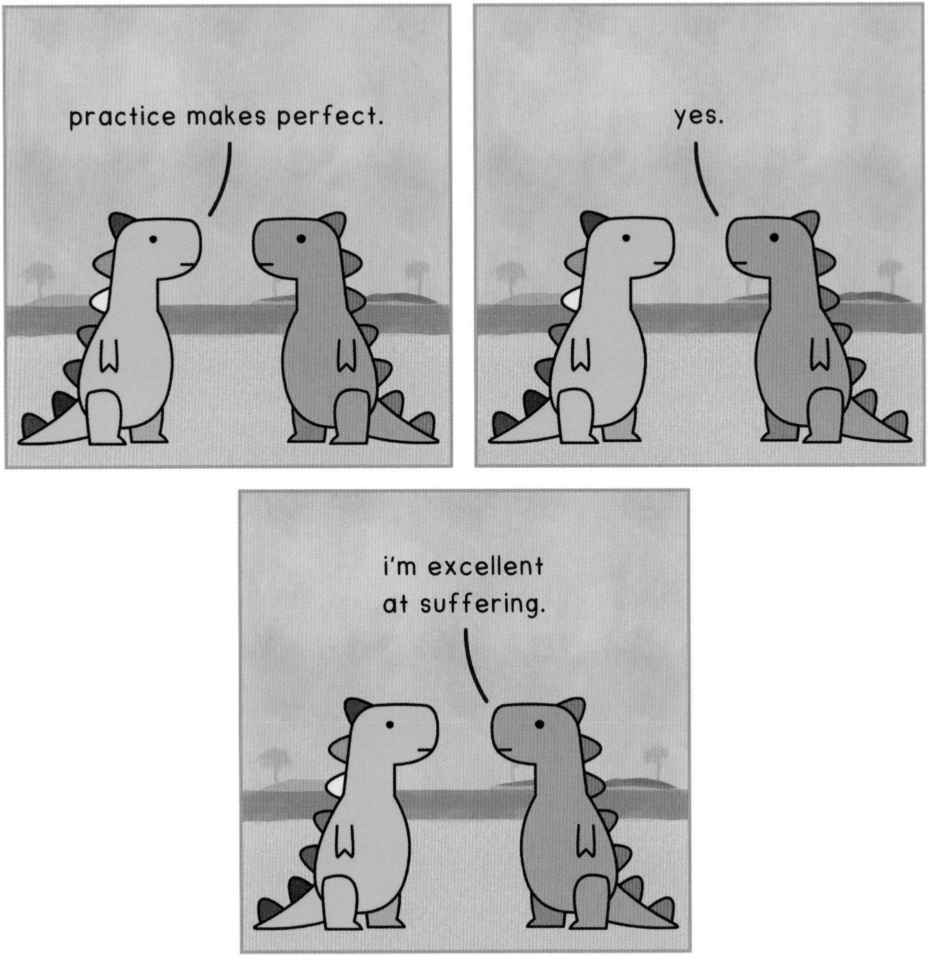
practice makes perfect.
yes.
i'm excellent
at suffering.

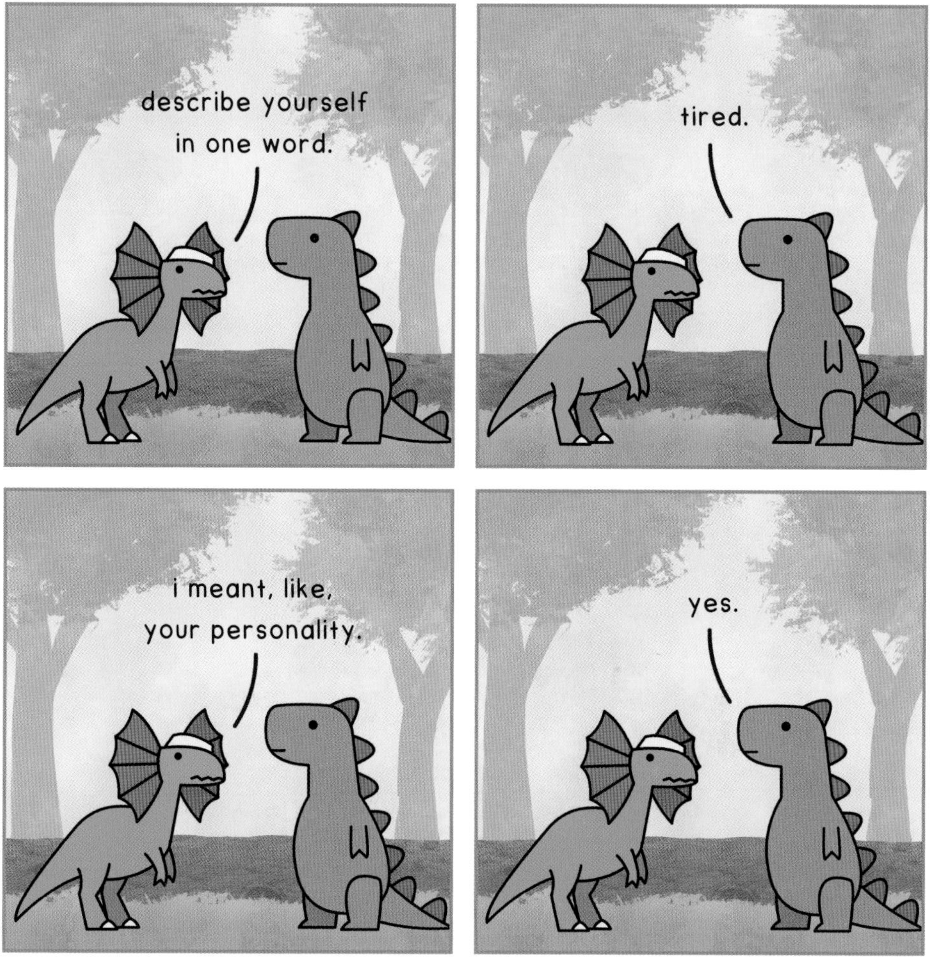
describe yourself in one word.
tired.
i meant, like, your personality.
yes.

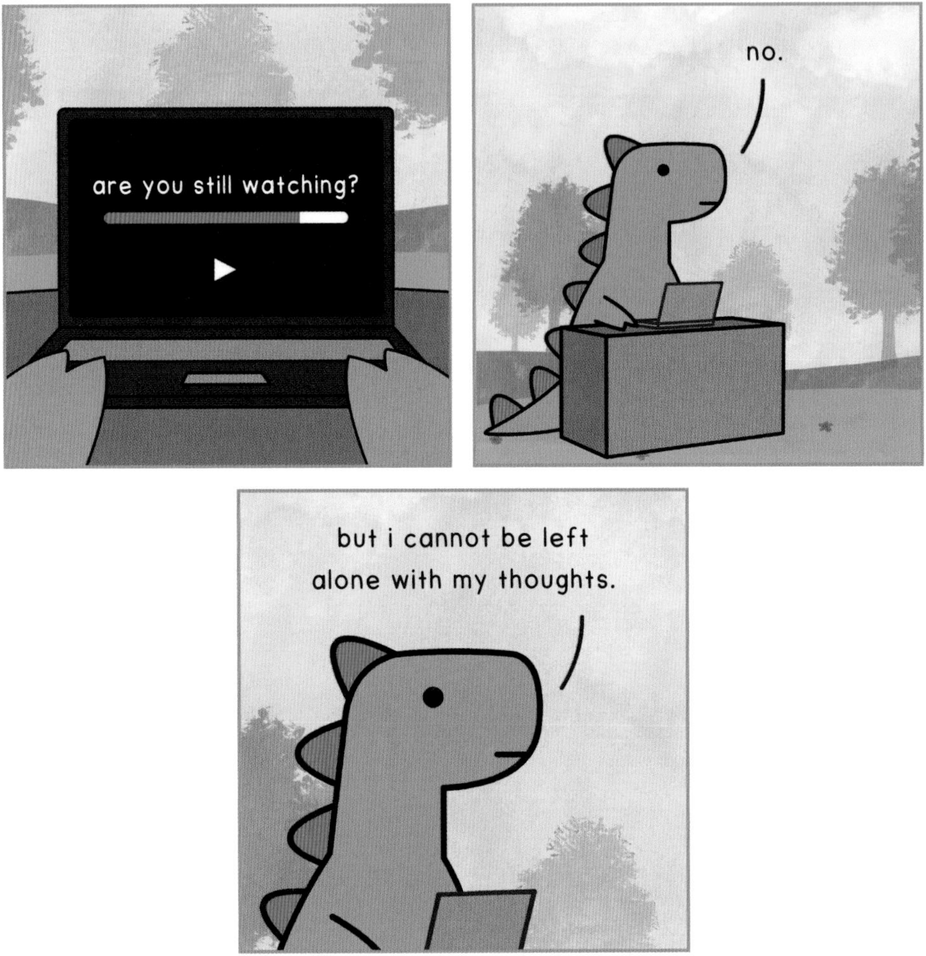
are you still watching?
no.
but i cannot be left alone with my thoughts.

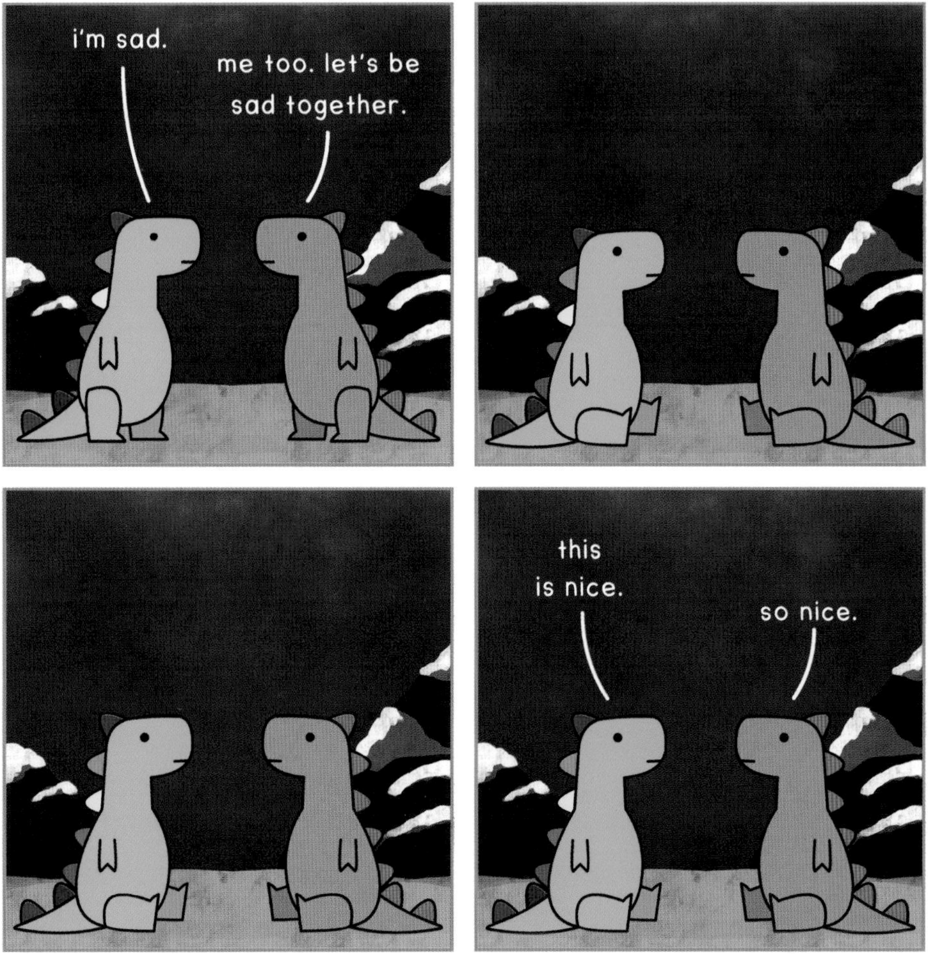
i'm sad.
me too. let's be sad together.
this is nice.
so nice.

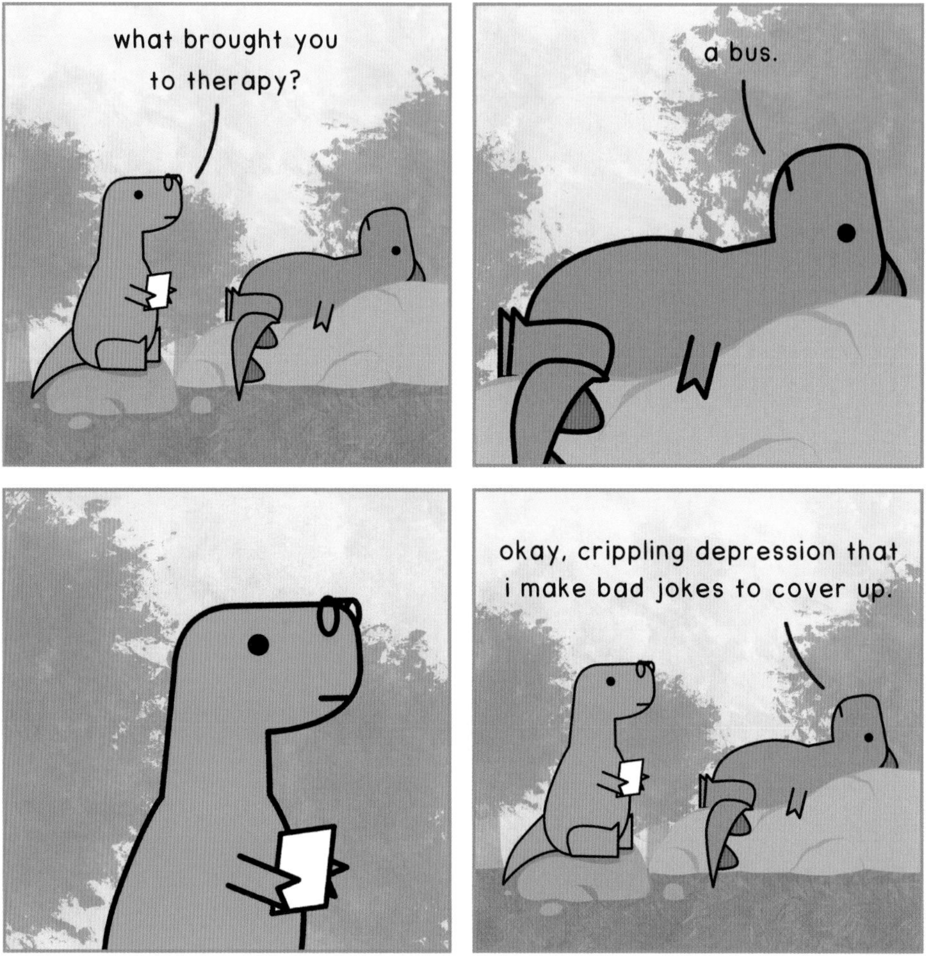
what brought you to therapy?
a bus.
okay, crippling depression that i make bad jokes to cover up.

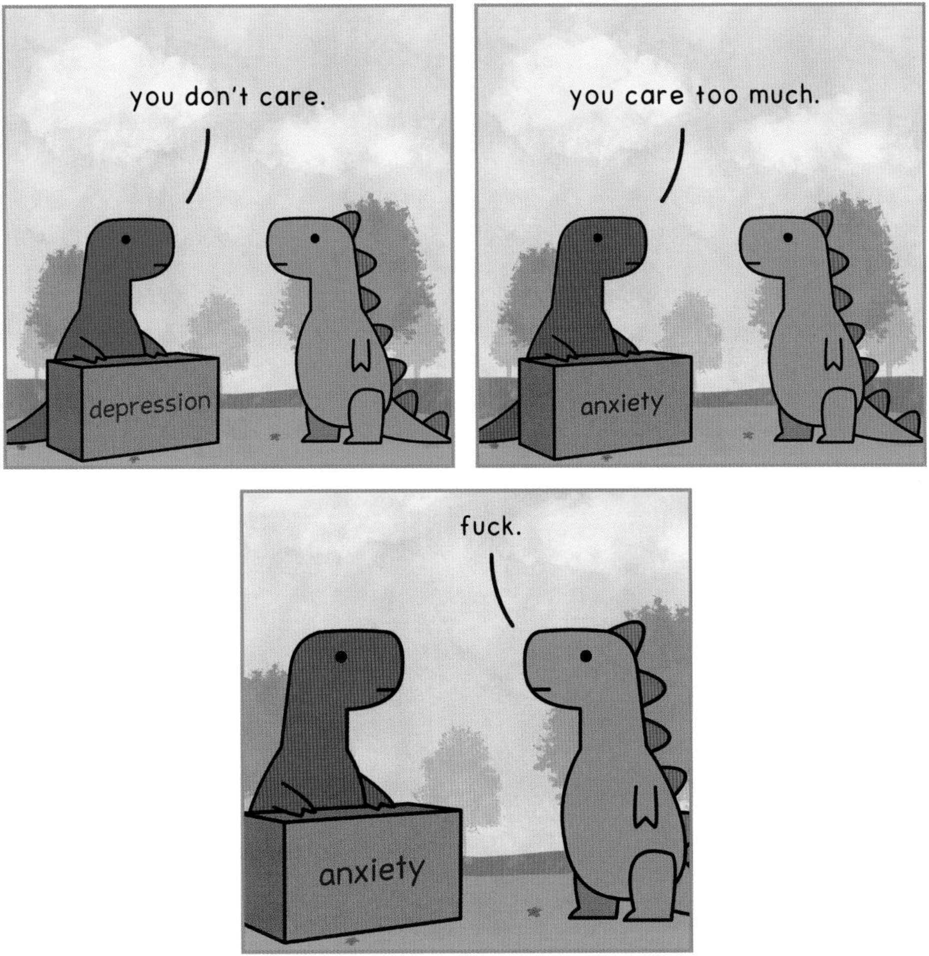
you don't care.
depression
you care too much.
anxiety
fuck.
anxiety

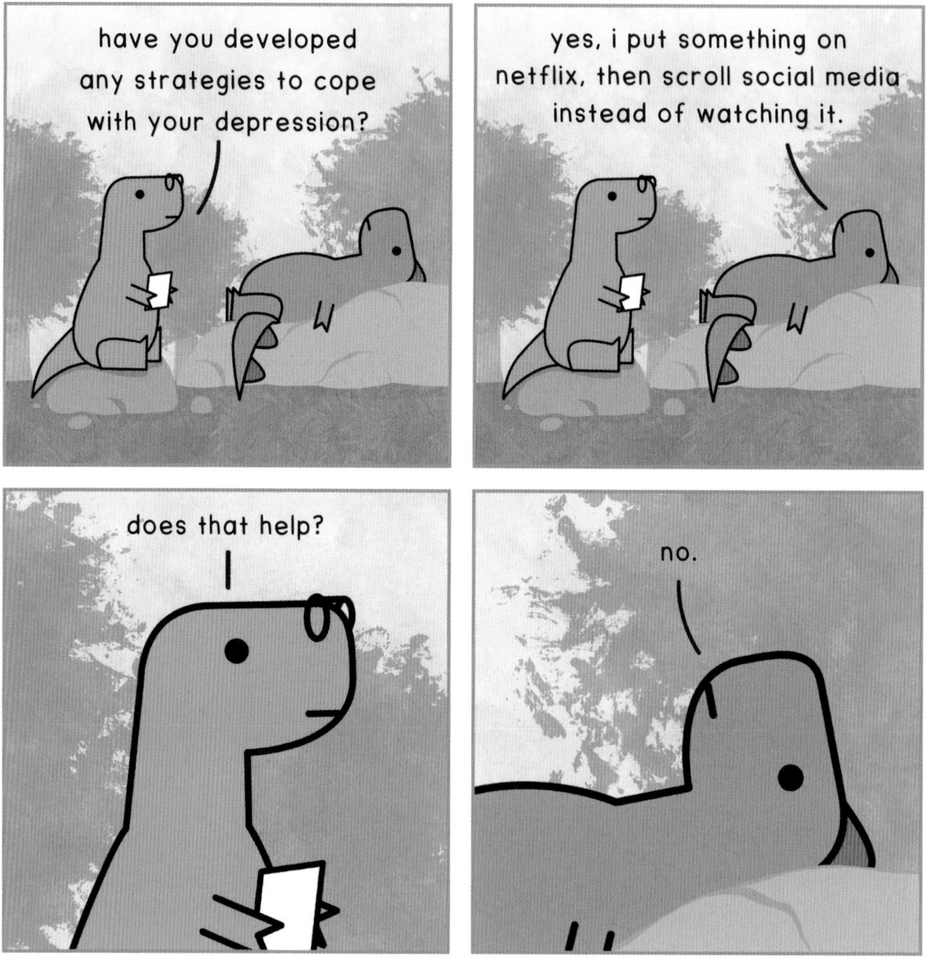
have you developed any strategies to cope with your depression?
yes, i put something on netflix, then scroll social media instead of watching it.
does that help?
no.

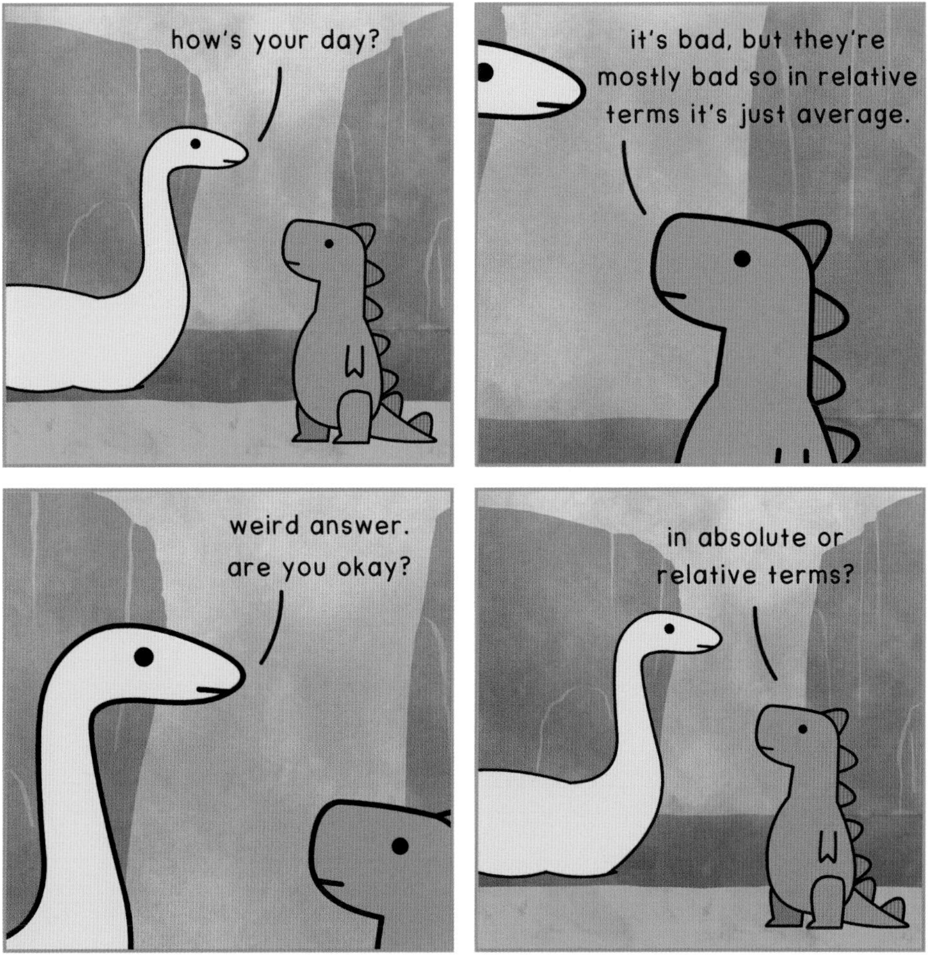
how's your day?
it's bad, but they're mostly bad so in relative terms it's just average.
weird answer. are you okay?
in absolute or relative terms?

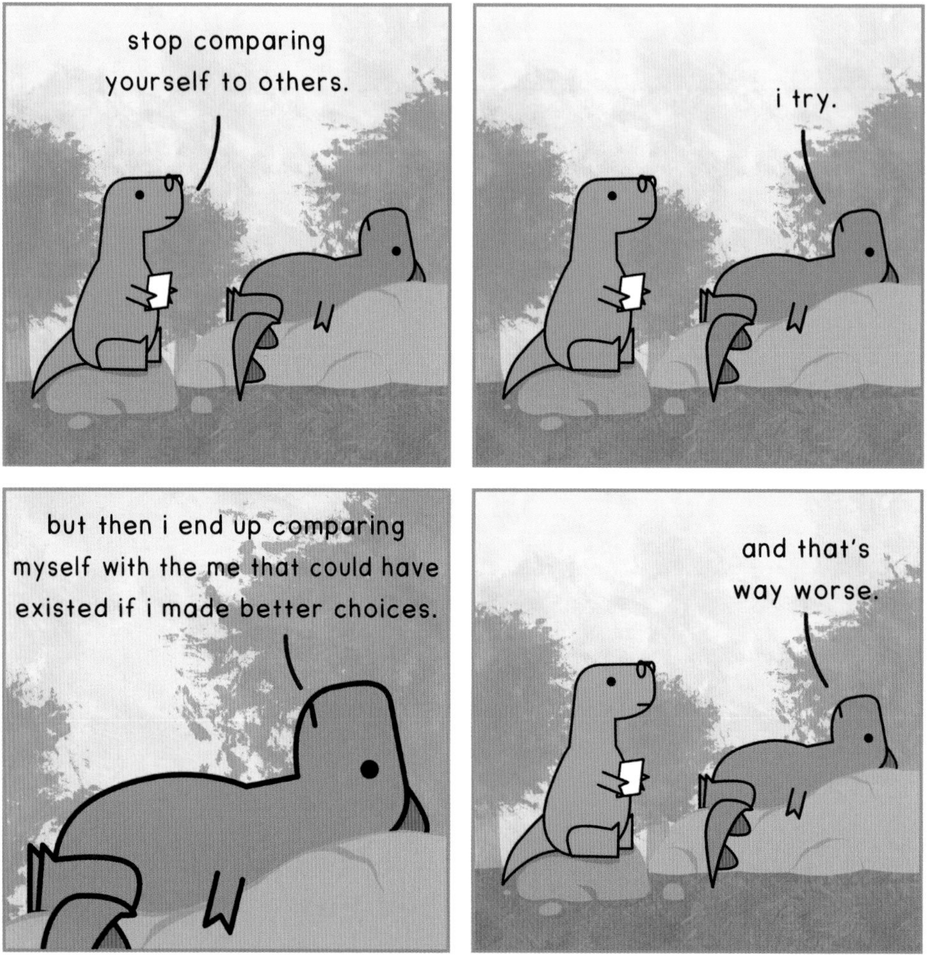
stop comparing yourself to others.
i try.
but then i end up comparing myself with the me that could have existed if i made better choices.
and that's way worse.

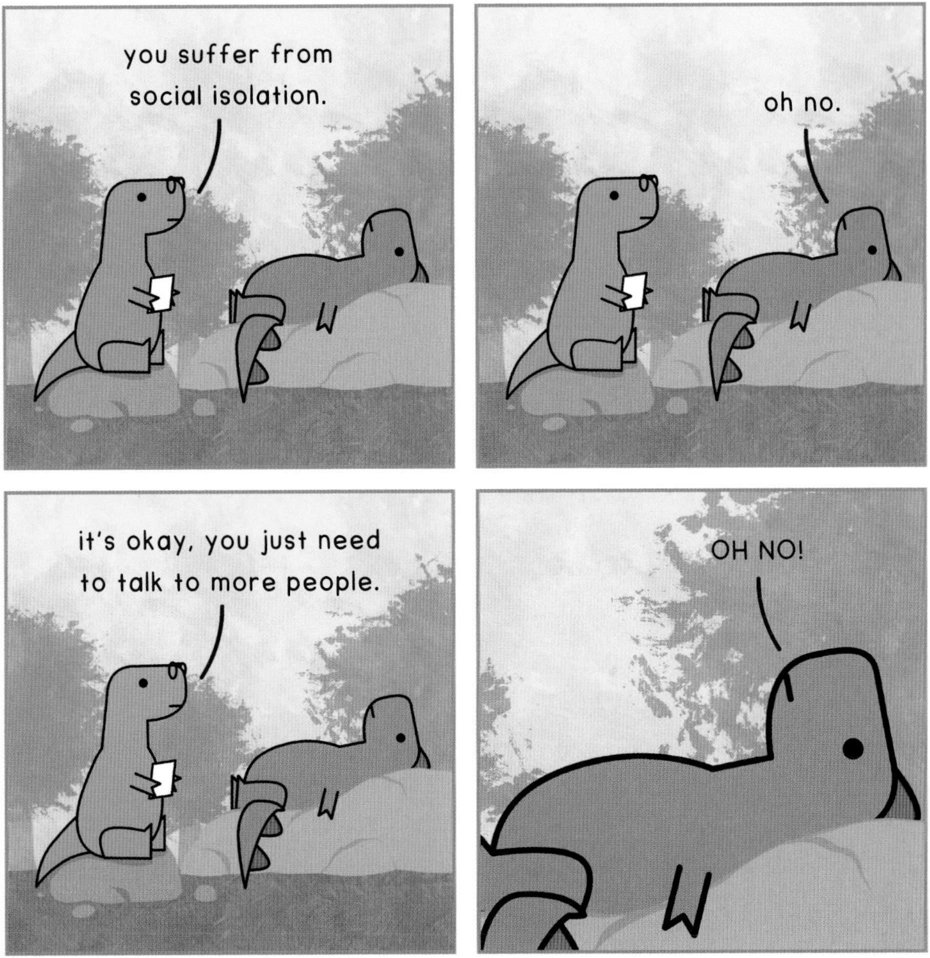
you suffer from social isolation.
oh no.
it's okay, you just need to talk to more people.
OH NO!

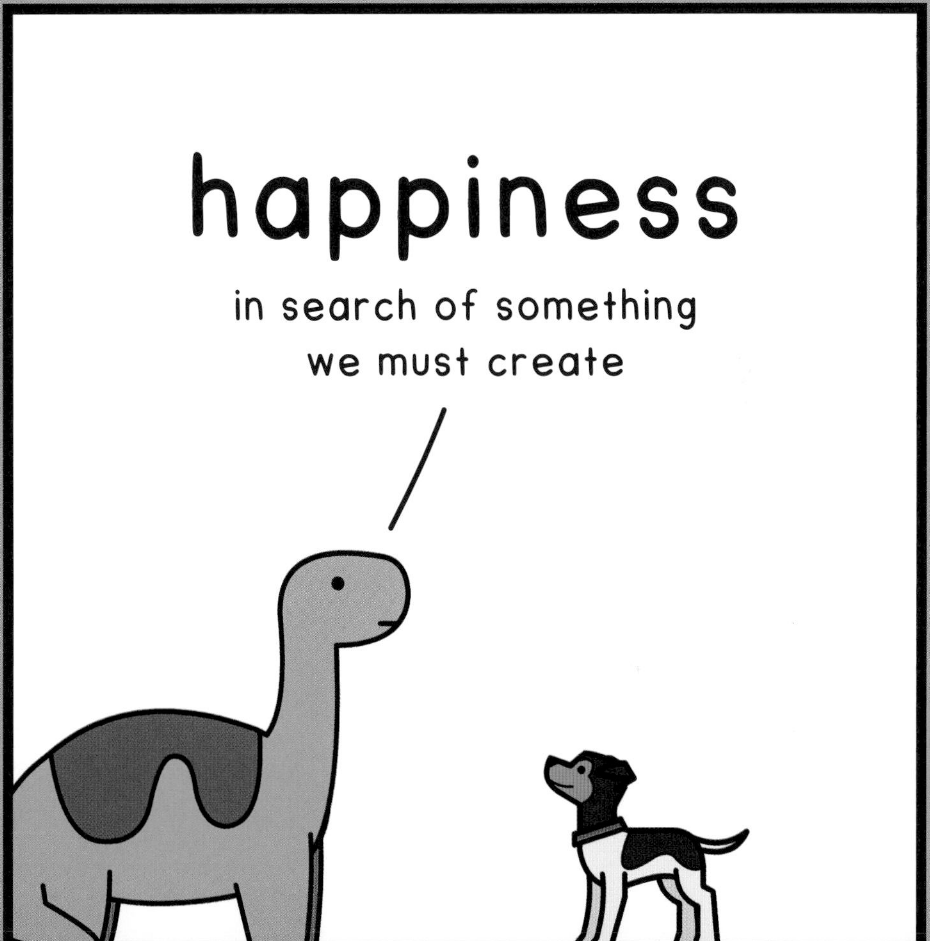
happiness
in search of something
we must create

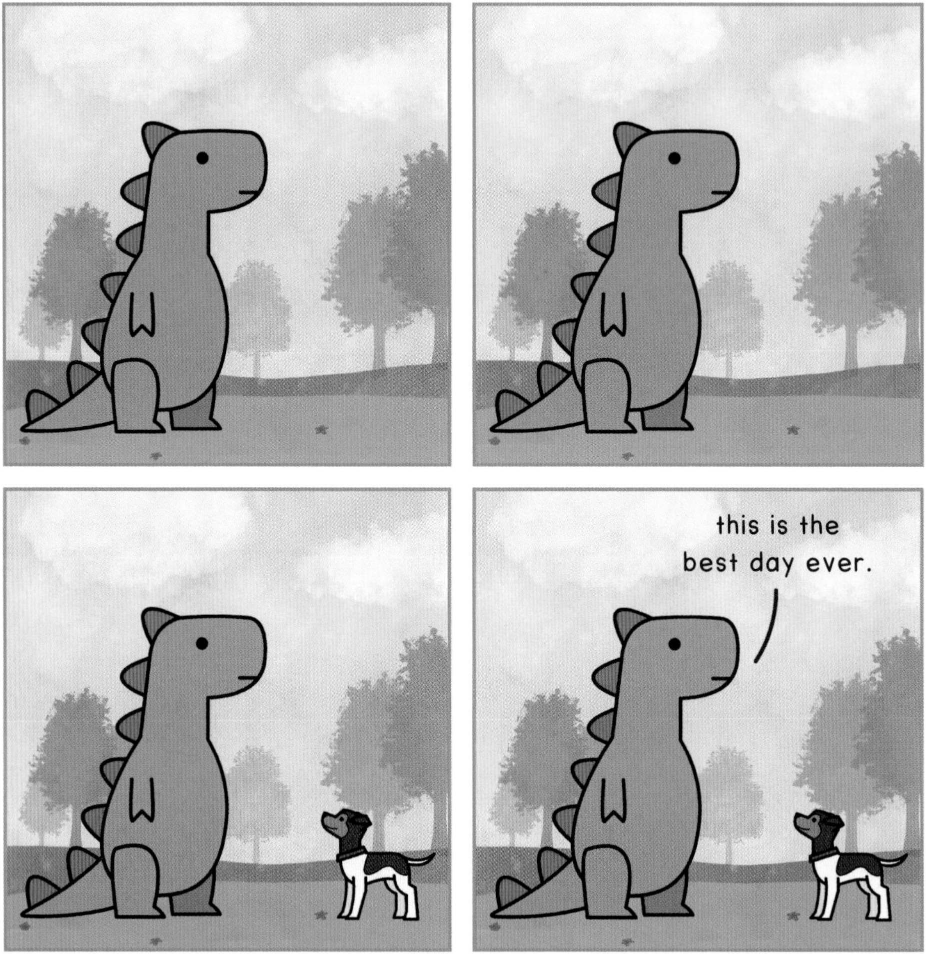
this is the
best day ever.

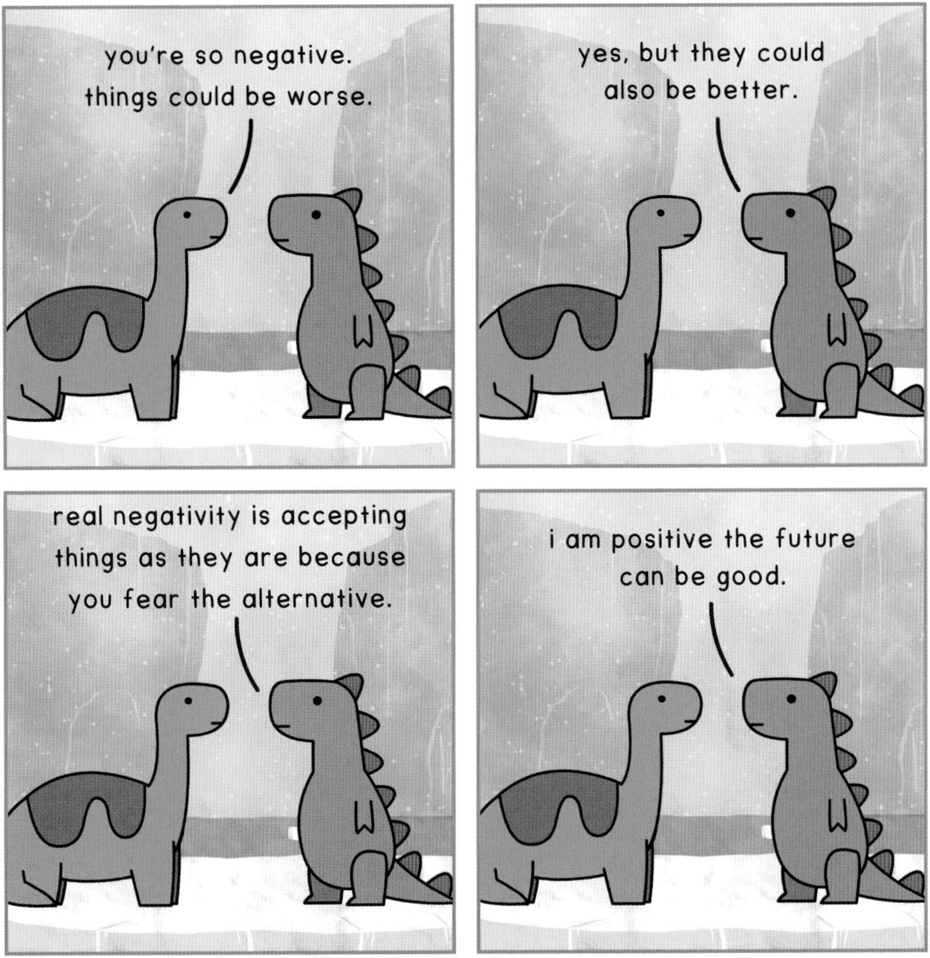
you're so negative. things could be worse.
yes, but they could also be better.
real negativity is accepting things as they are because you fear the alternative.
i am positive the future can be good.

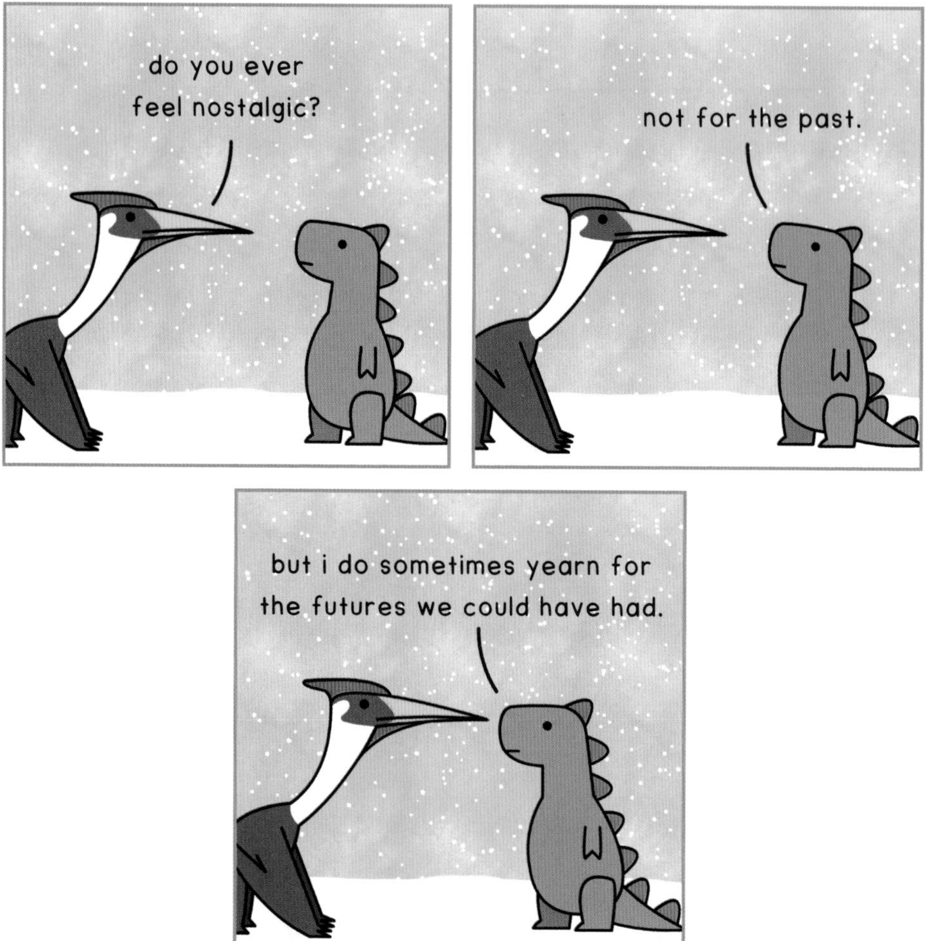
do you ever feel nostalgic?
not for the past.
but i do sometimes yearn for the futures we could have had.

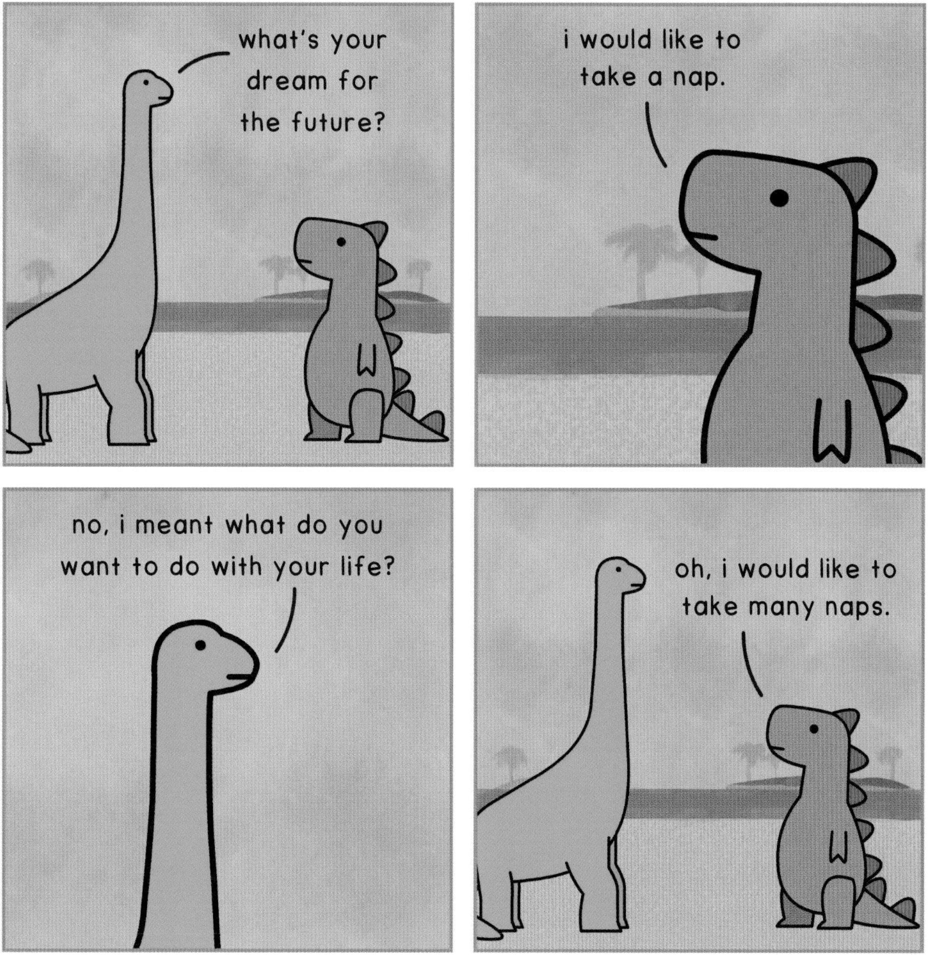
what's your dream for the future?
i would like to take a nap.
no, i meant what do you want to do with your life?
oh, i would like to take many naps.

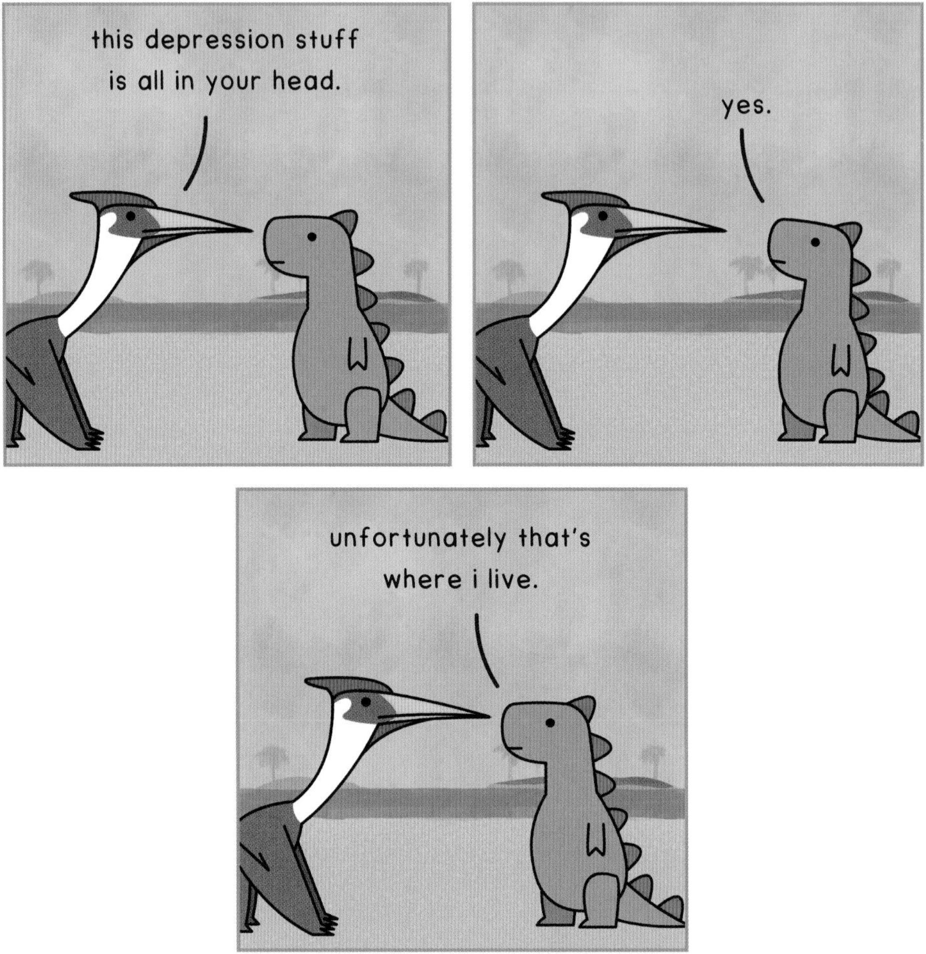
this depression stuff is all in your head.
yes.
unfortunately that's where i live.

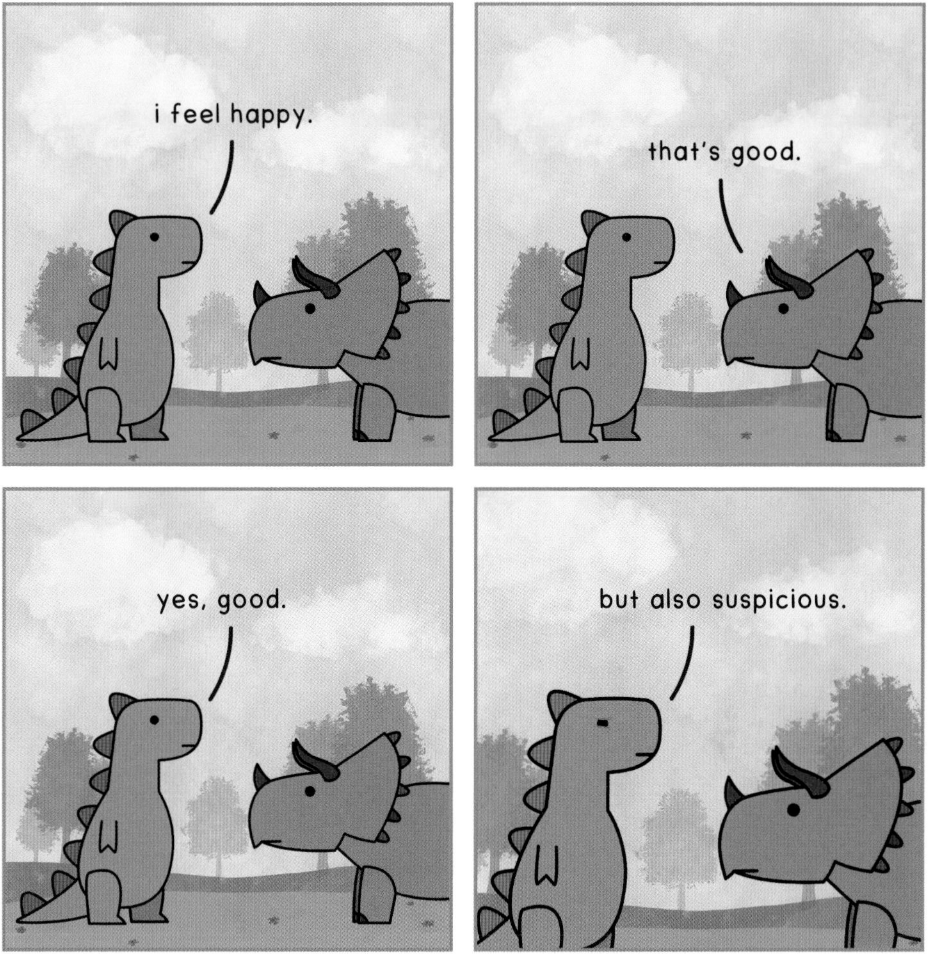
i feel happy.
that's good.
yes, good.
but also suspicious.

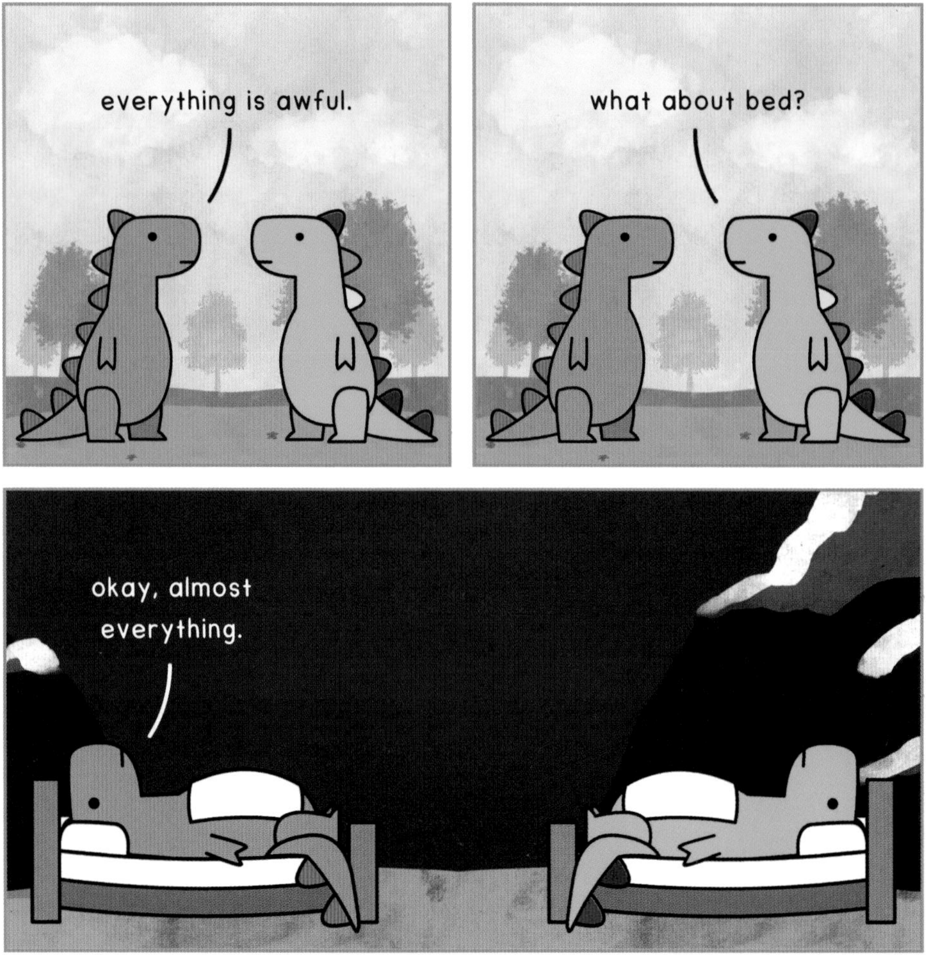
everything is awful.
what about bed?
okay, almost
everything.

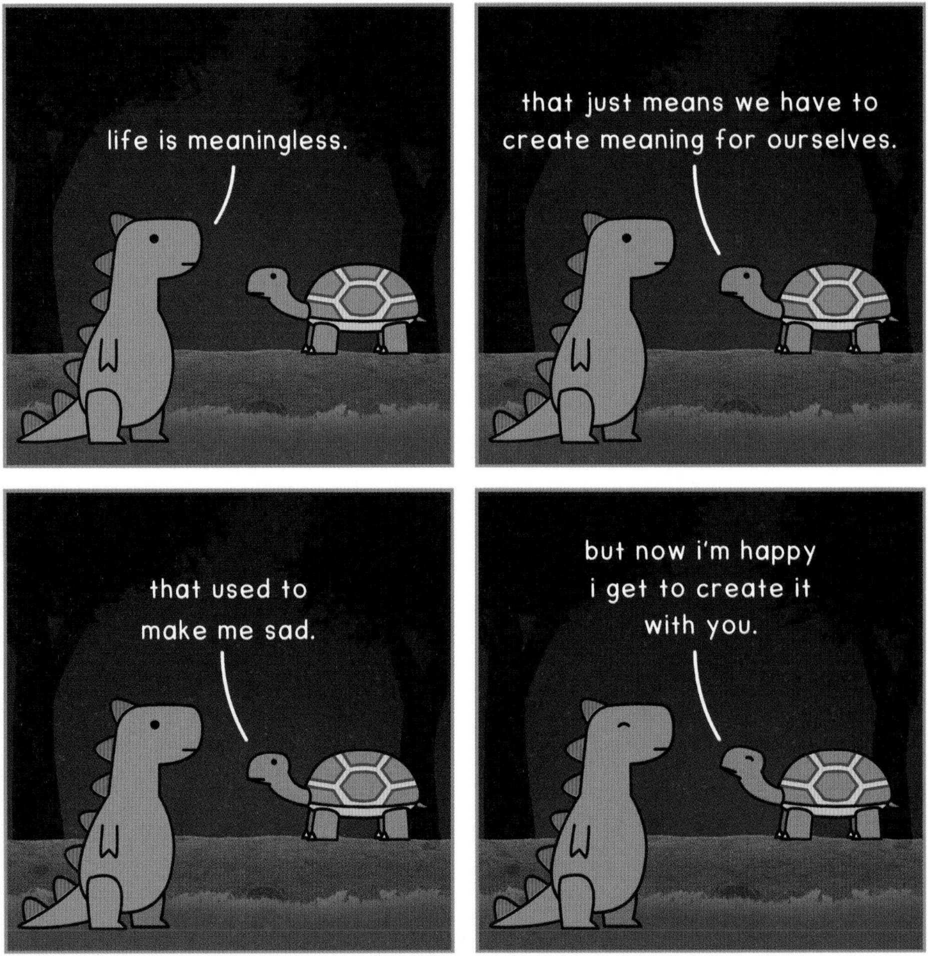
life is meaningless.
that just means we have to create meaning for ourselves.
that used to make me sad.
but now i'm happy i get to create it with you.

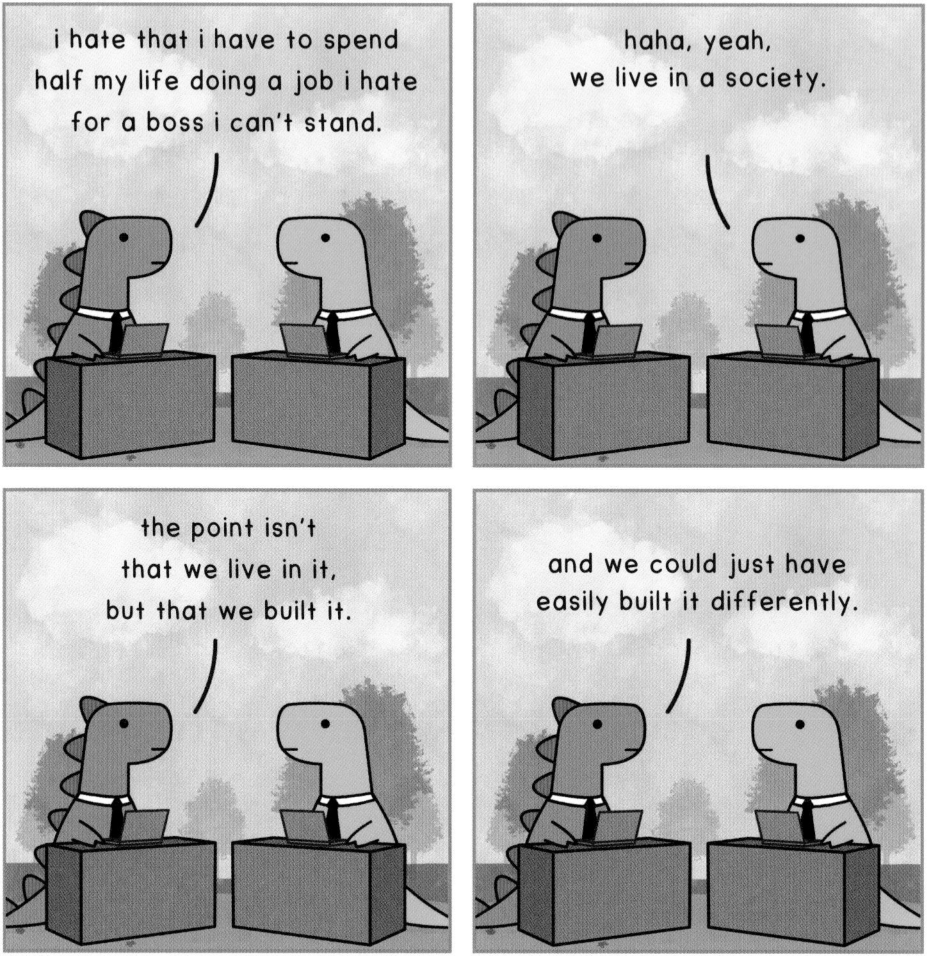
i hate that i have to spend half my life doing a job i hate for a boss i can't stand.
haha, yeah, we live in a society.
the point isn't that we live in it, but that we built it.
and we could just have easily built it differently.

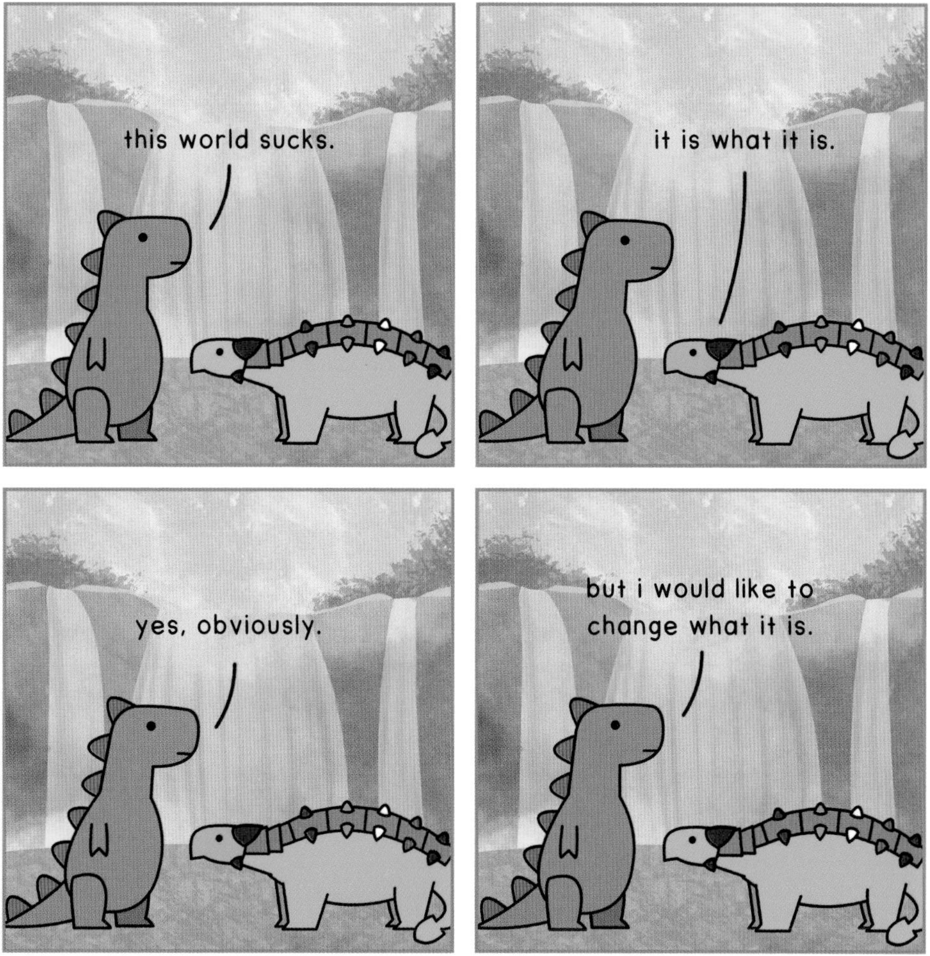
this world sucks.
it is what it is.
yes, obviously.
but i would like to change what it is.

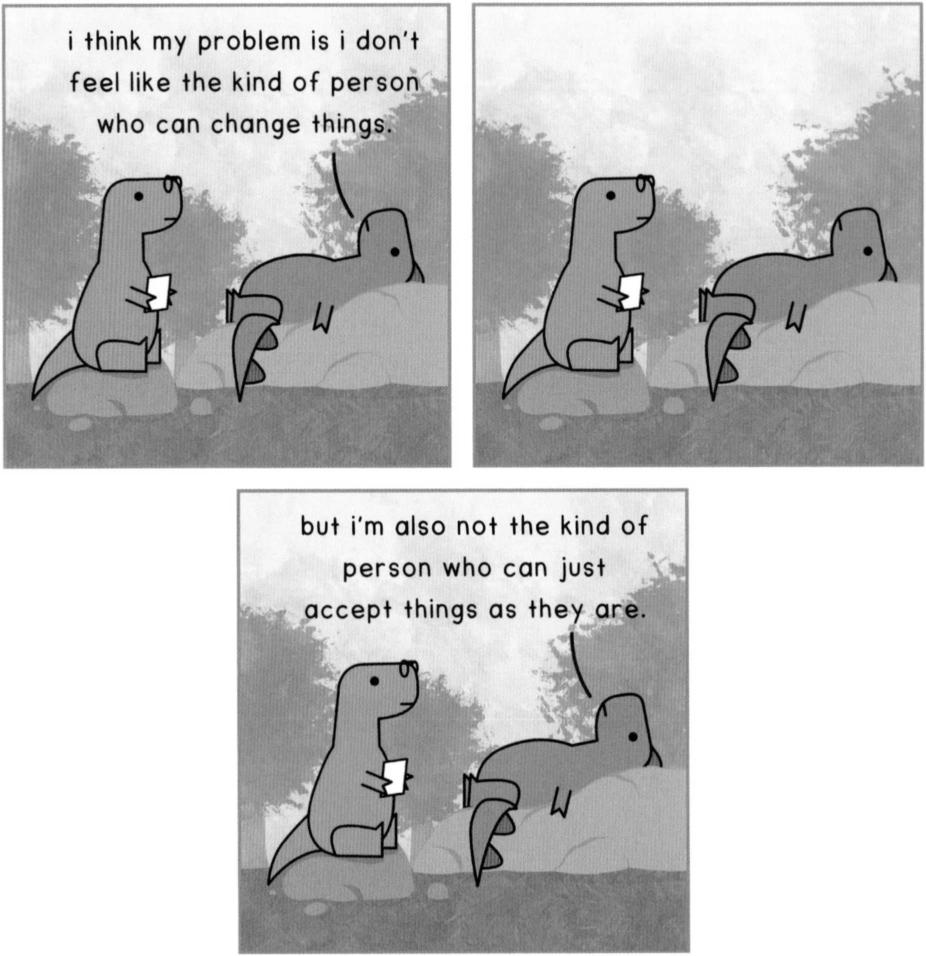
i think my problem is i don't feel like the kind of person who can change things.
but i'm also not the kind of person who can just accept things as they are.

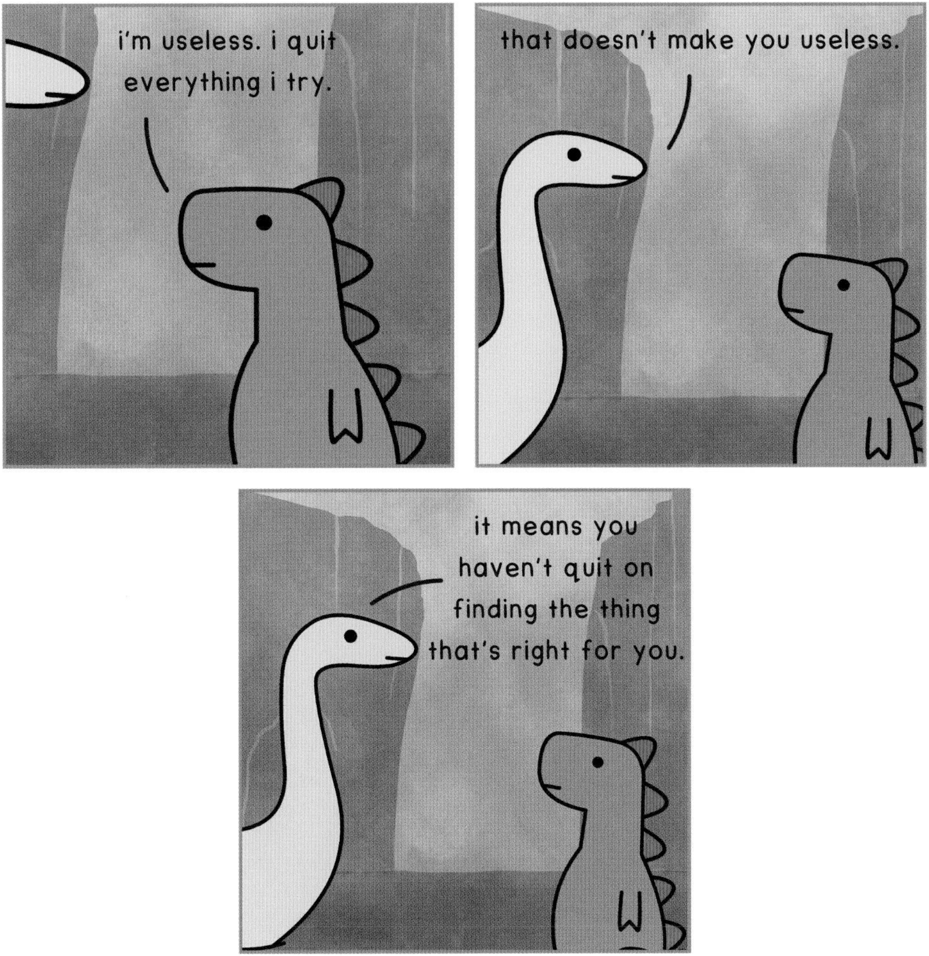
i'm useless. i quit everything i try.
that doesn't make you useless.
it means you haven't quit on finding the thing that's right for you.

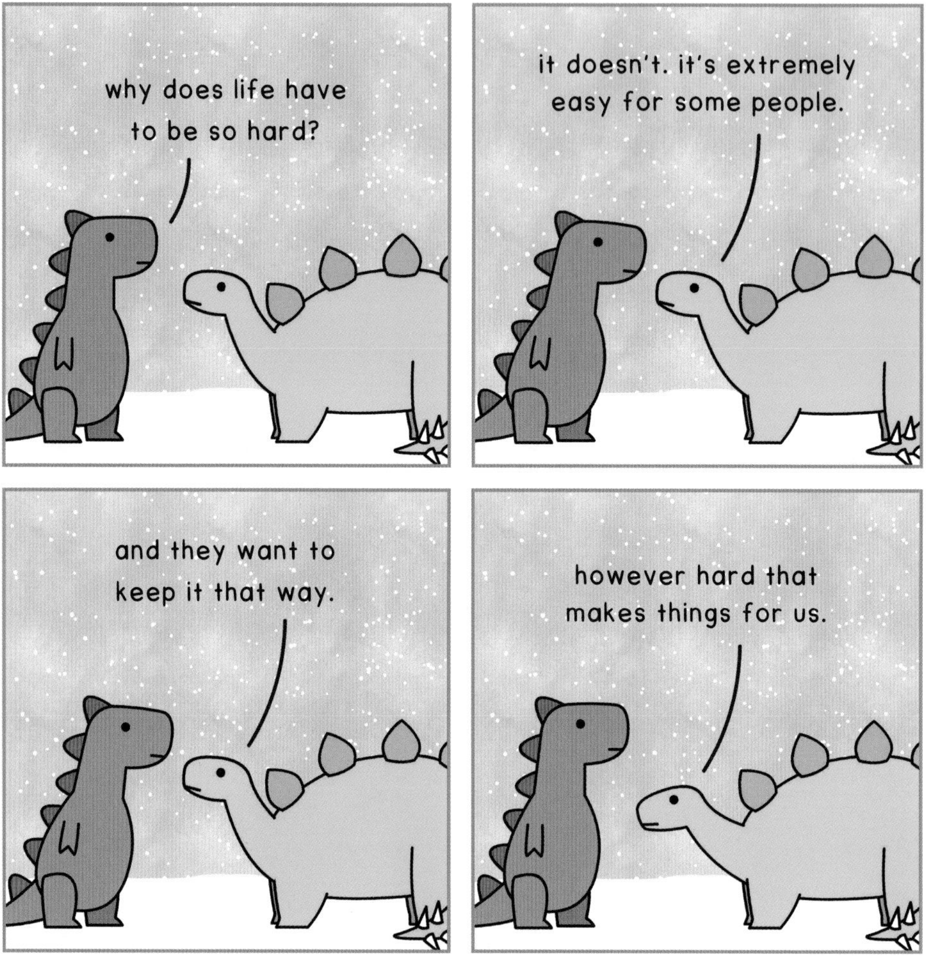
why does life have to be so hard?
it doesn't. it's extremely easy for some people.
and they want to keep it that way.
however hard that makes things for us.

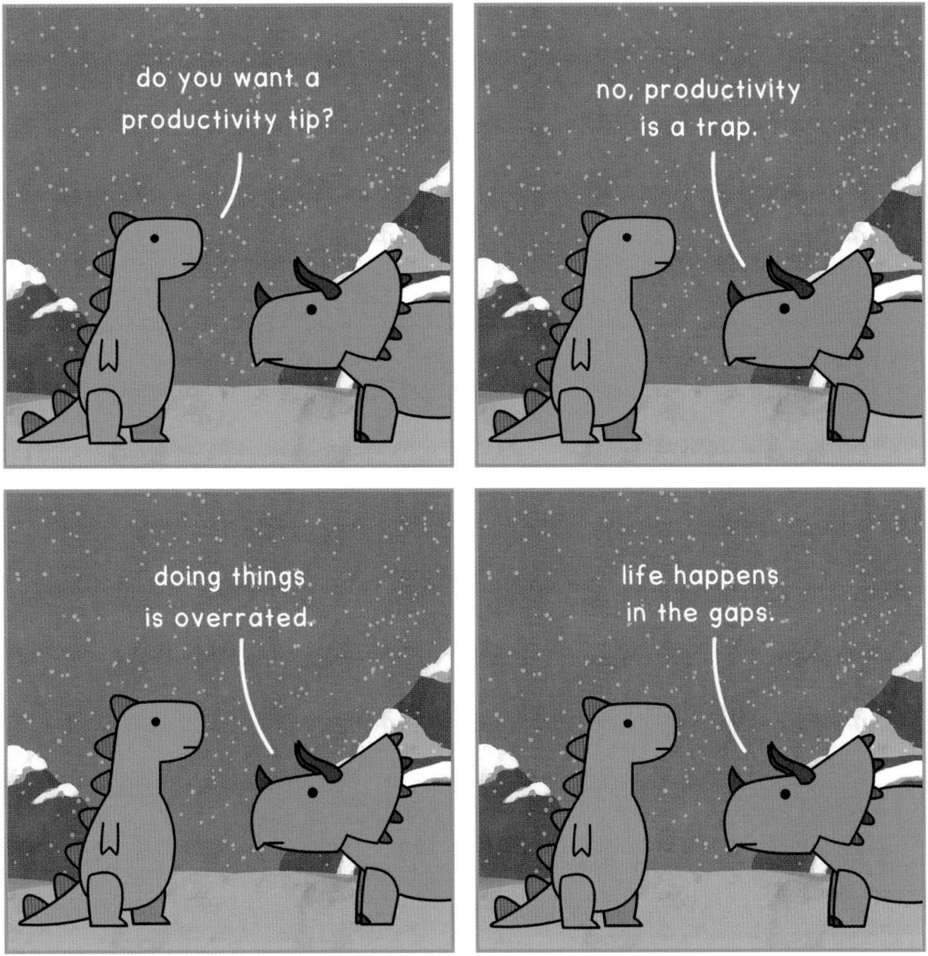
do you want a productivity tip?
no, productivity is a trap.
doing things is overrated.
life happens in the gaps.

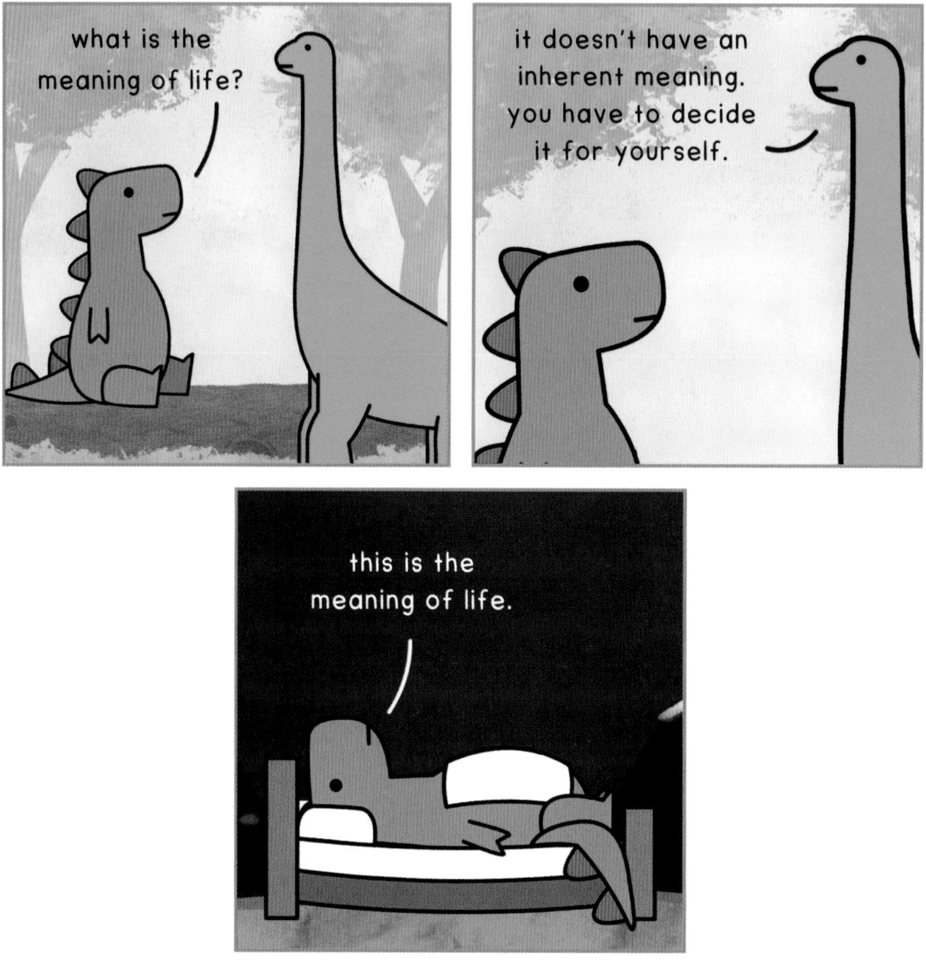
what is the meaning of life?
it doesn't have an inherent meaning. you have to decide it for yourself.
this is the meaning of life.

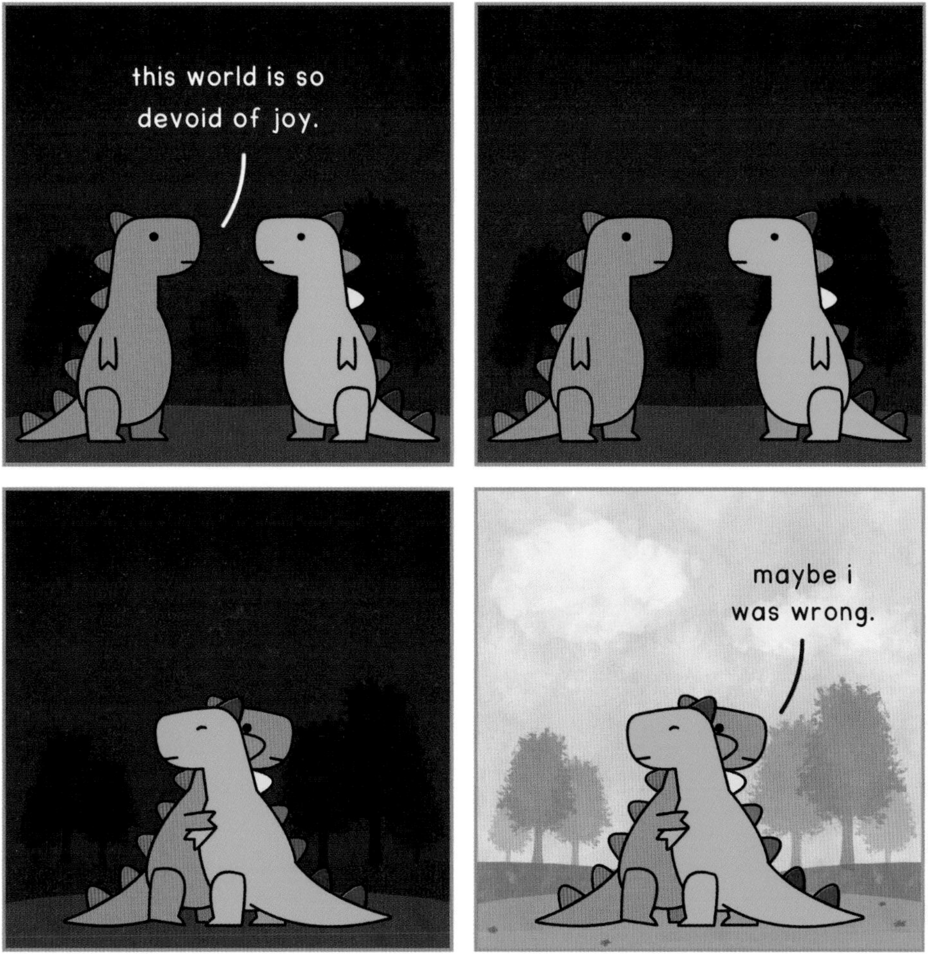
this world is so devoid of joy.
maybe i was wrong.

relationships

it's clichéd to be cynical about love

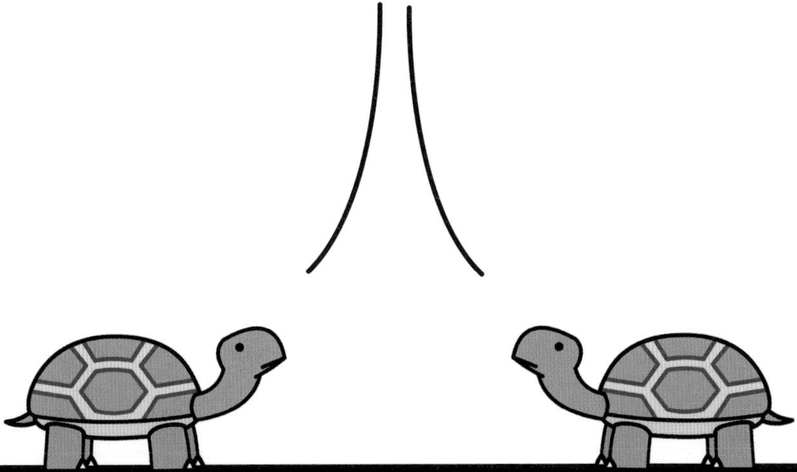

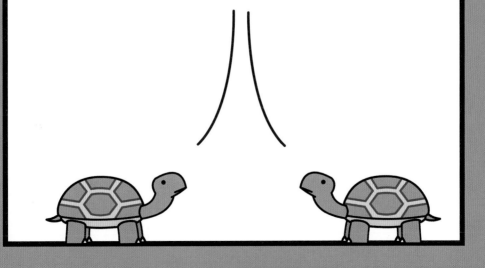

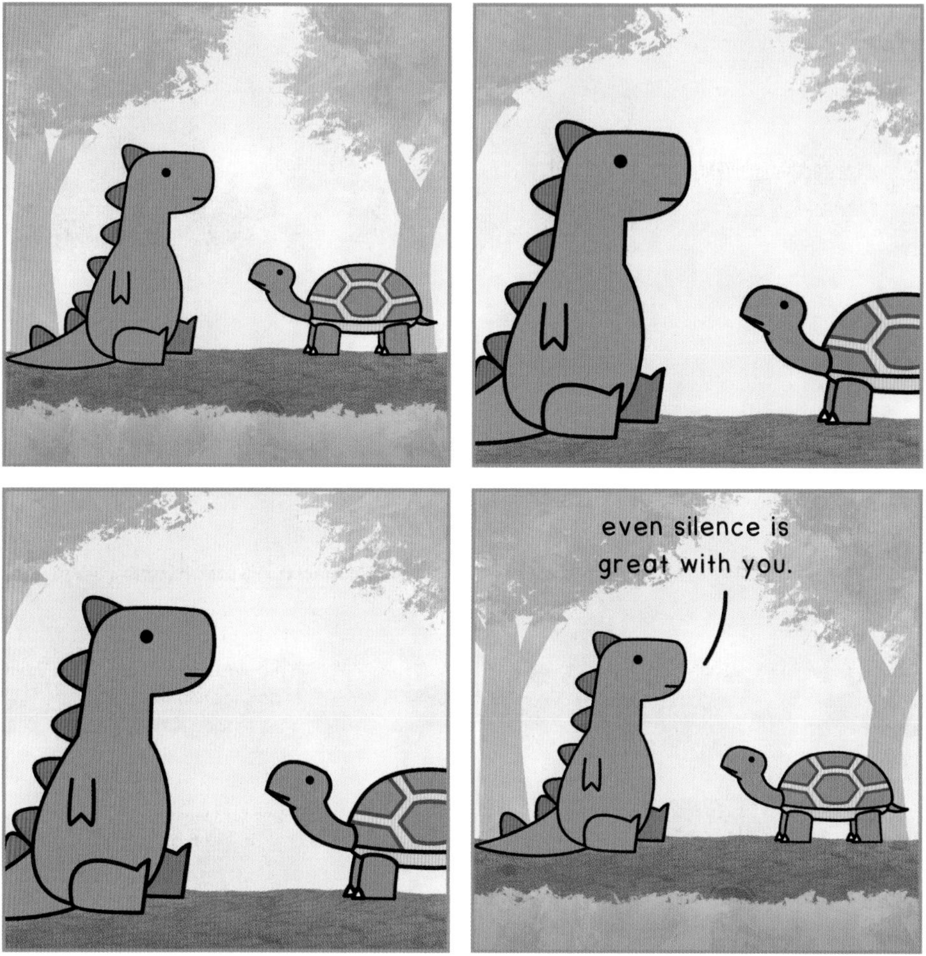
even silence is
great with you.

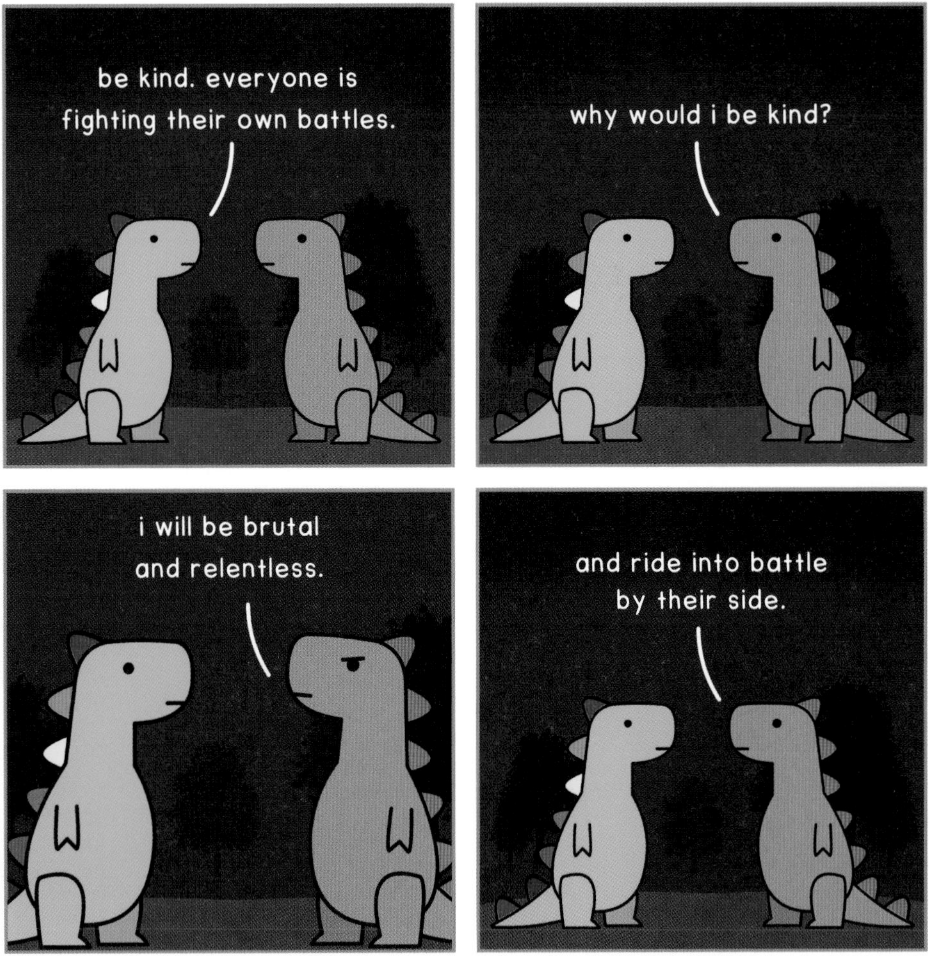
be kind. everyone is fighting their own battles.
why would i be kind?
i will be brutal and relentless.
and ride into battle by their side.

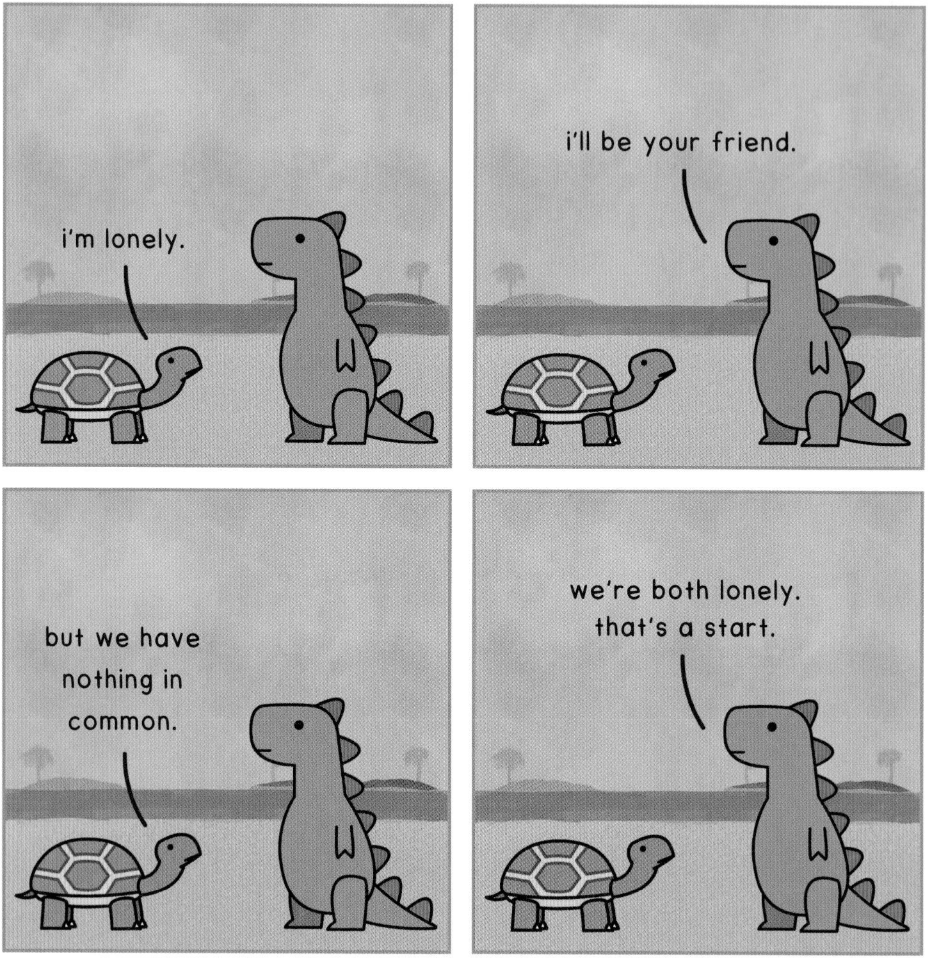
i'm lonely.
i'll be your friend.
but we have nothing in common.
we're both lonely. that's a start.

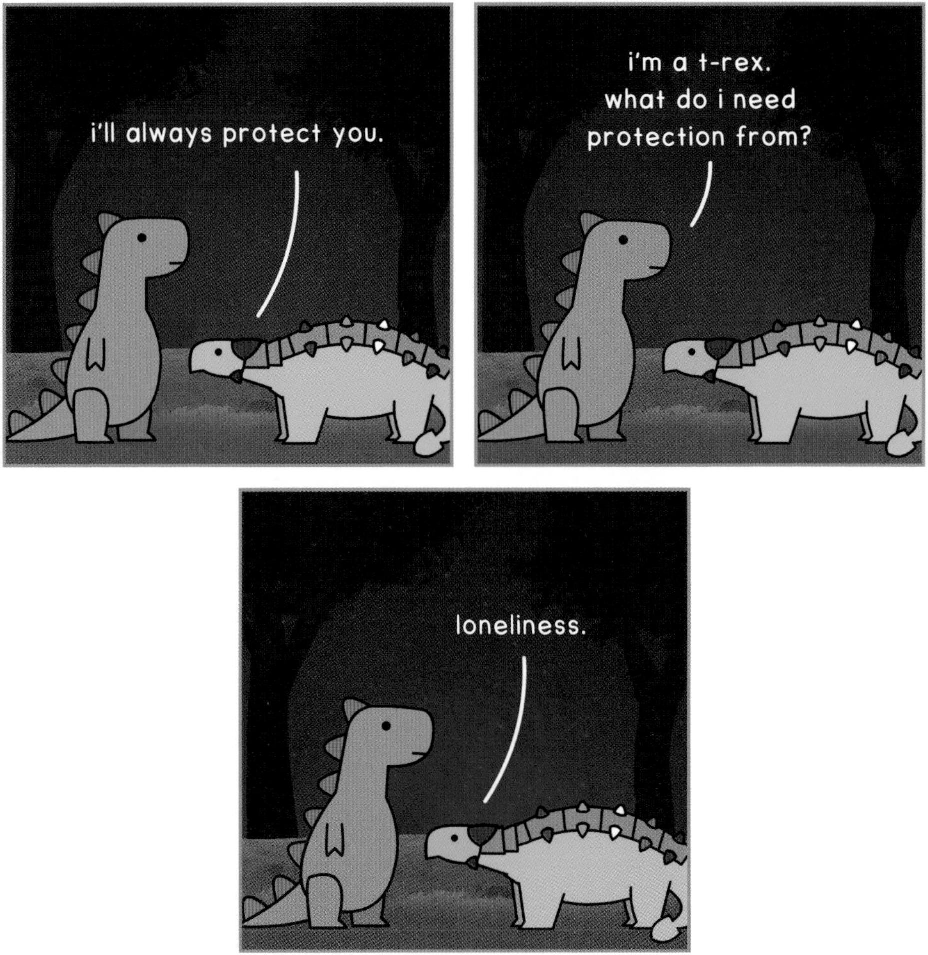
i'll always protect you.
i'm a t-rex.
what do i need
protection from?
loneliness.

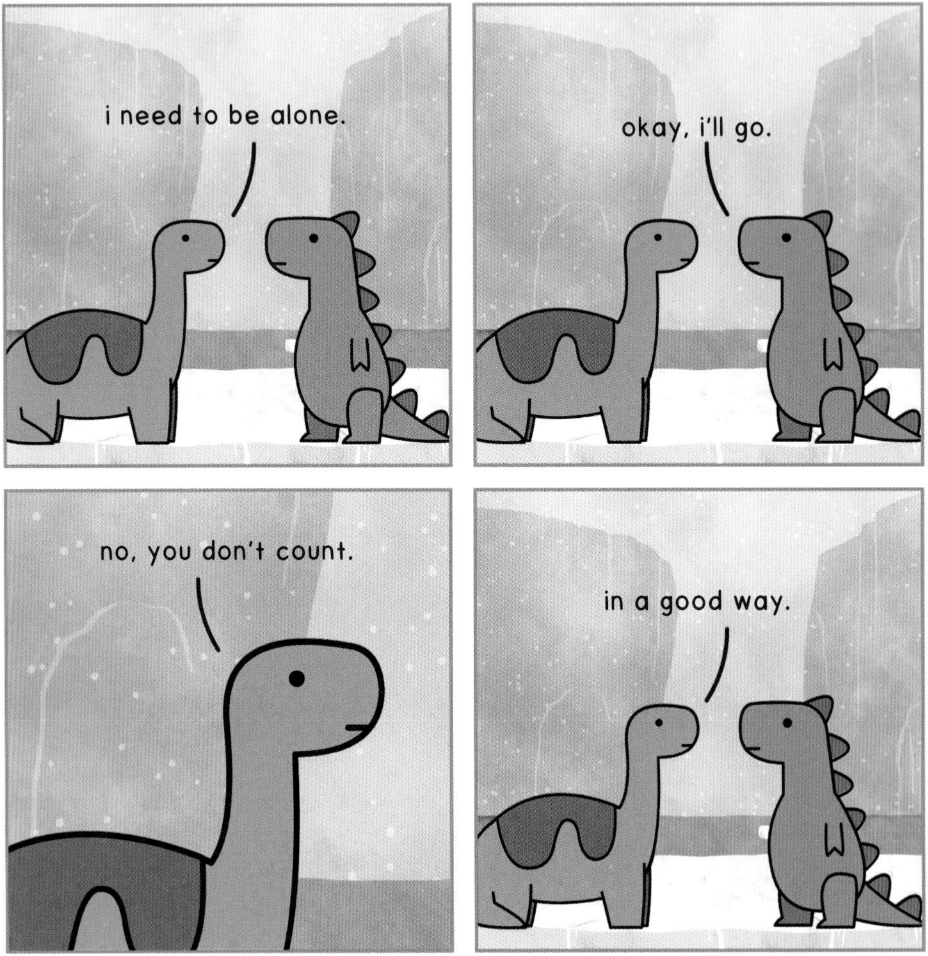
i need to be alone.
okay, i'll go.
no, you don't count.
in a good way.

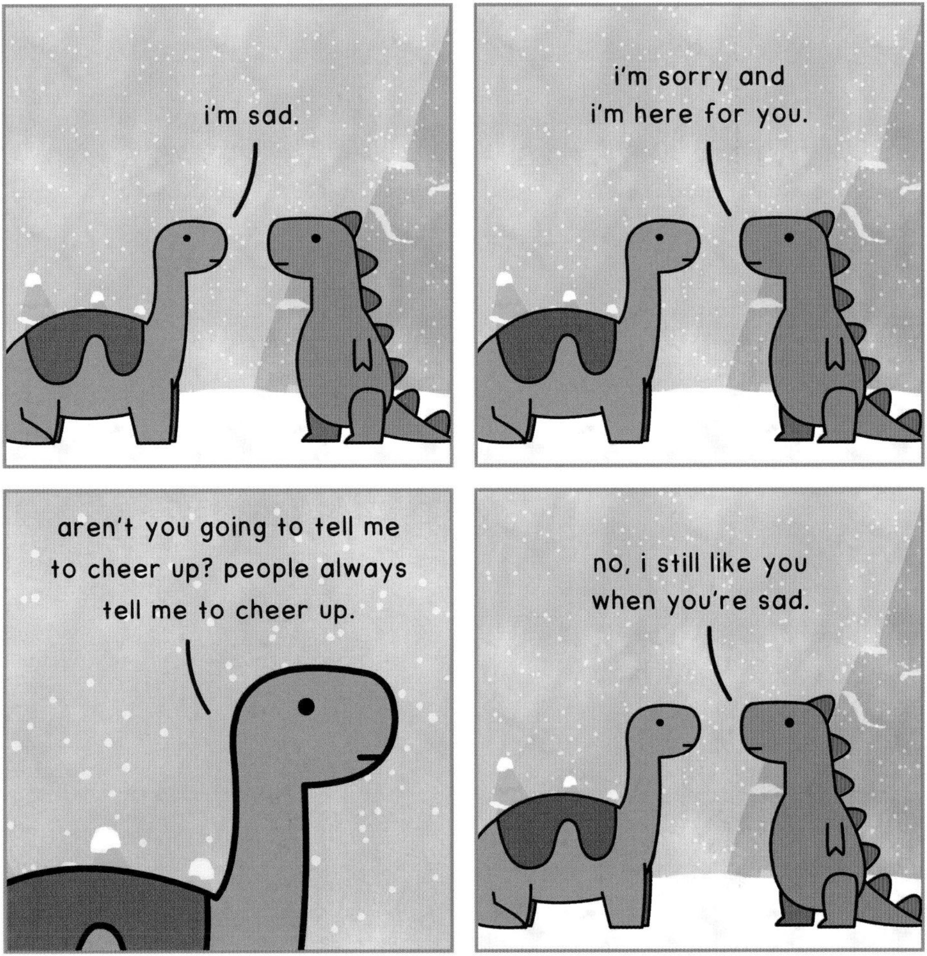
i'm sad.
i'm sorry and i'm here for you.
aren't you going to tell me to cheer up? people always tell me to cheer up.
no, i still like you when you're sad.

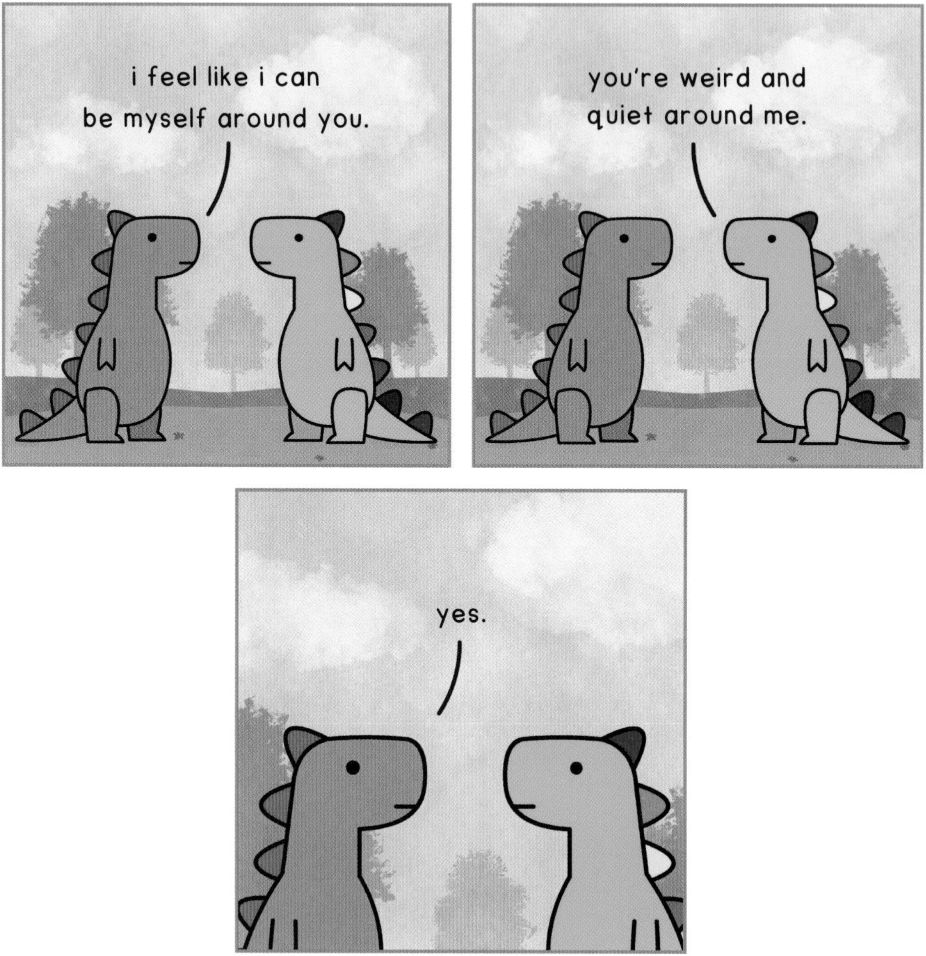
i feel like i can
be myself around you.
you're weird and
quiet around me.
yes.

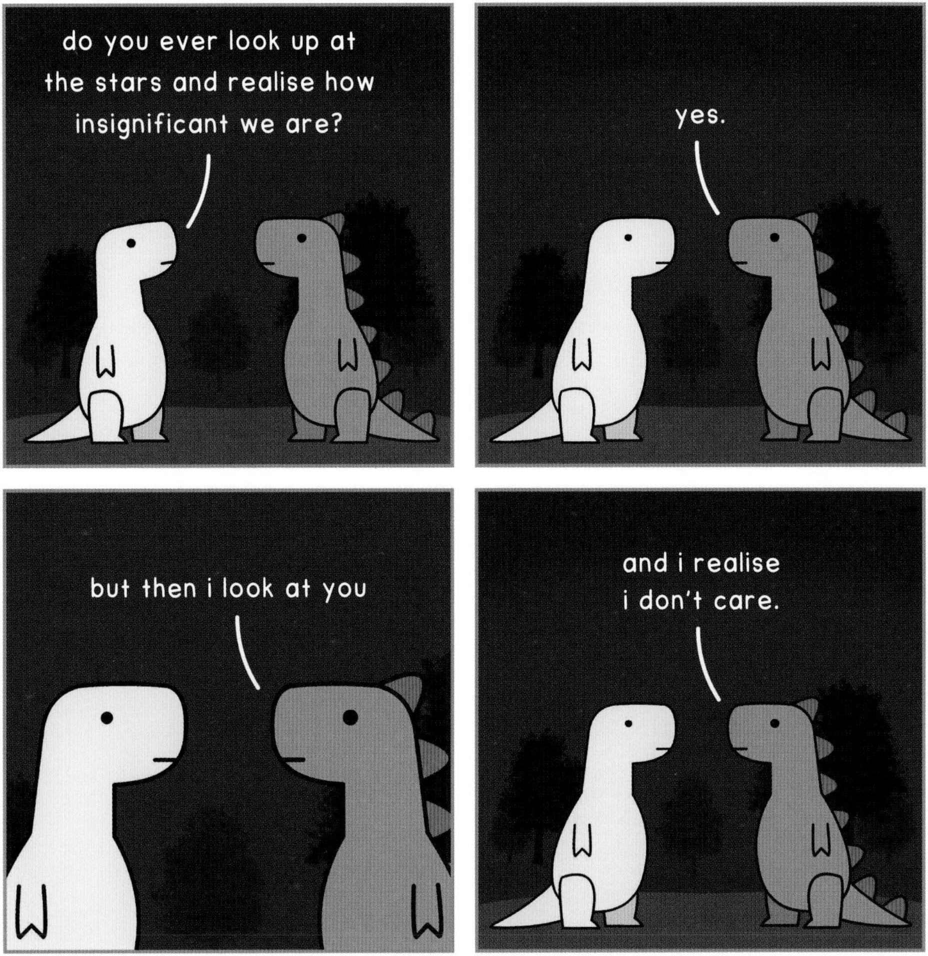
do you ever look up at the stars and realise how insignificant we are?
yes.
but then i look at you
and i realise i don't care.

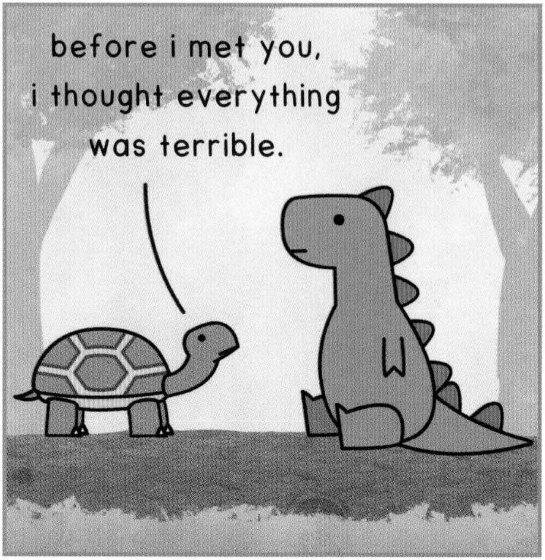
before i met you,
i thought everything
was terrible.

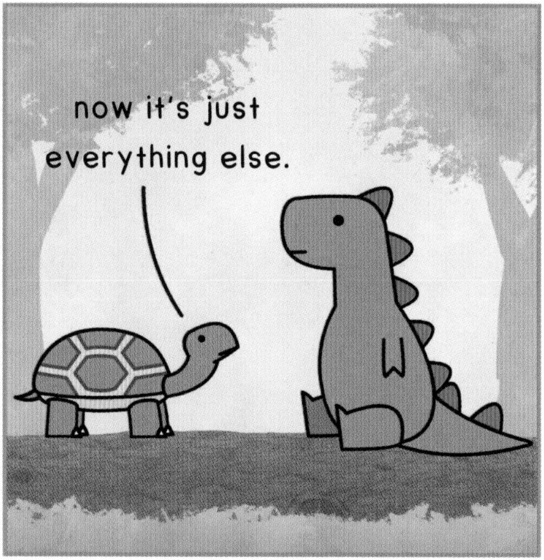
now it's just
everything else.

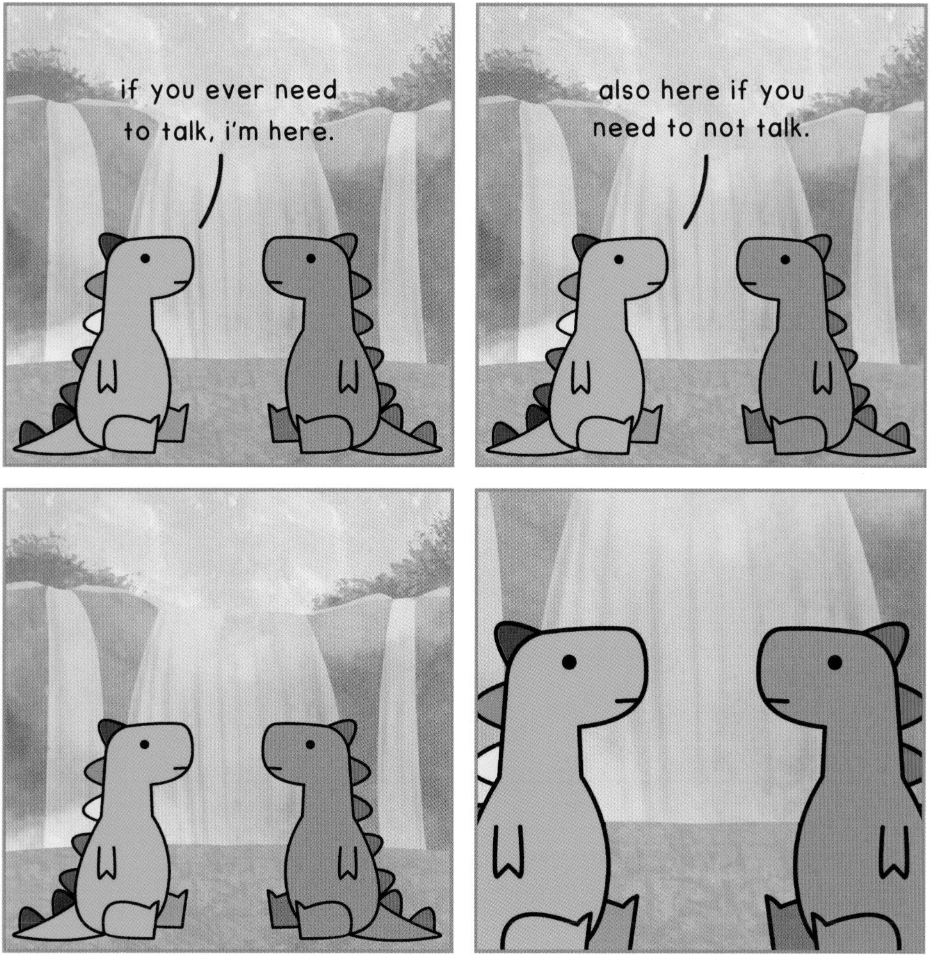
if you ever need to talk, i'm here.
also here if you need to not talk.

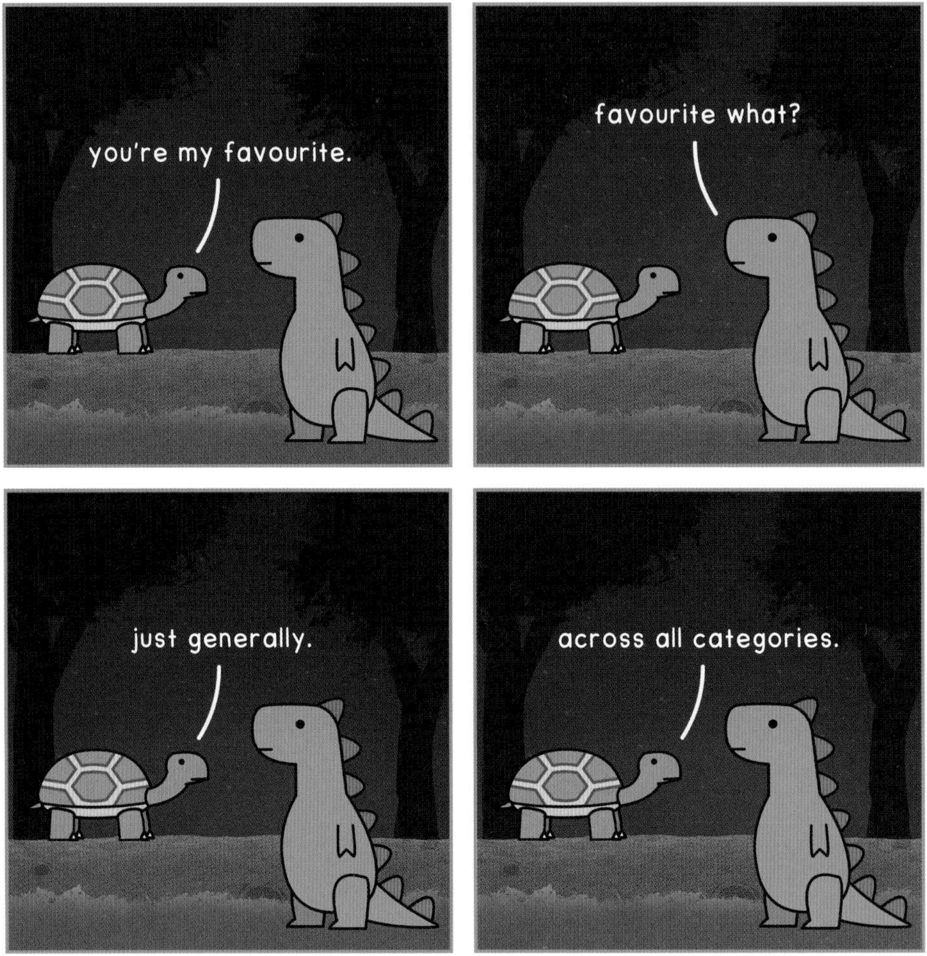
you're my favourite.
favourite what?
just generally.
across all categories.

usually when something bad happens, i go into my shell for protection.
but now i feel safer out here, with you.

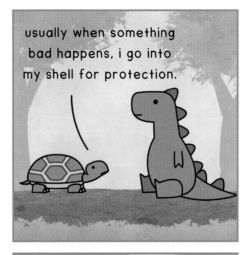

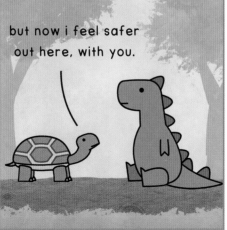

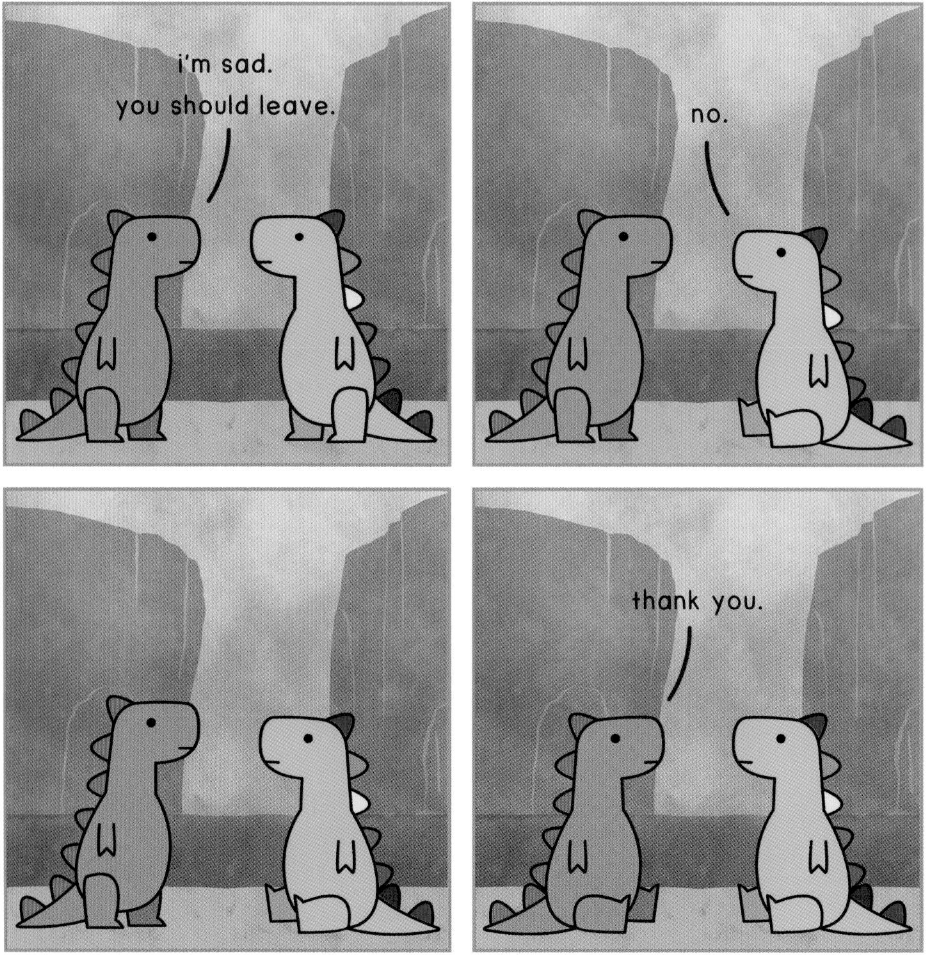
i'm sad.
you should leave.
no.
thank you.

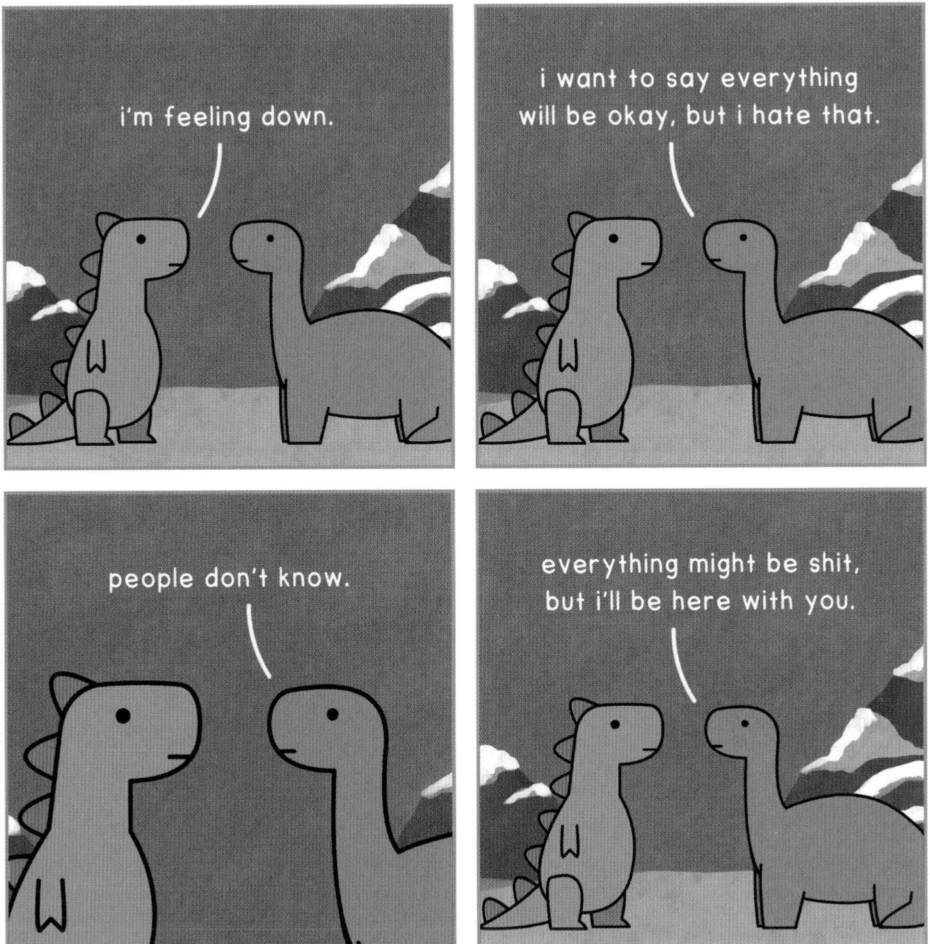
i'm feeling down.
i want to say everything will be okay, but i hate that.
people don't know.
everything might be shit, but i'll be here with you.

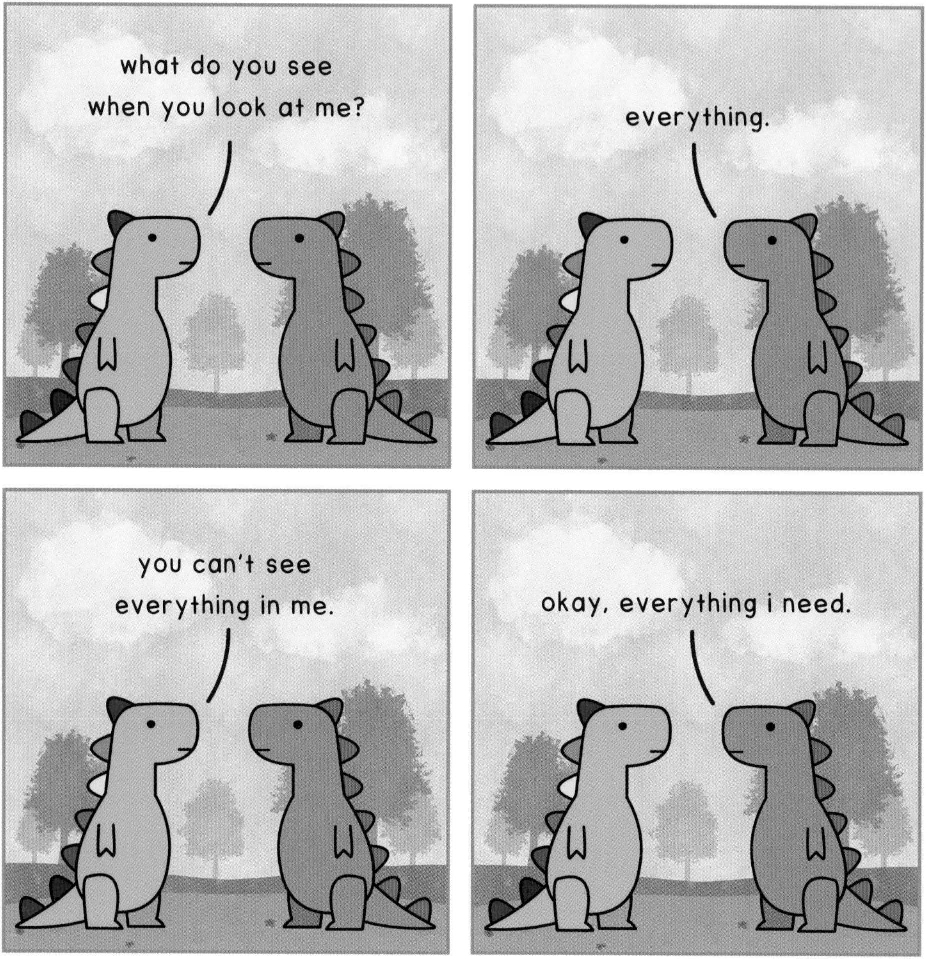
what do you see
when you look at me?
everything.
you can't see
everything in me.
okay, everything i need.

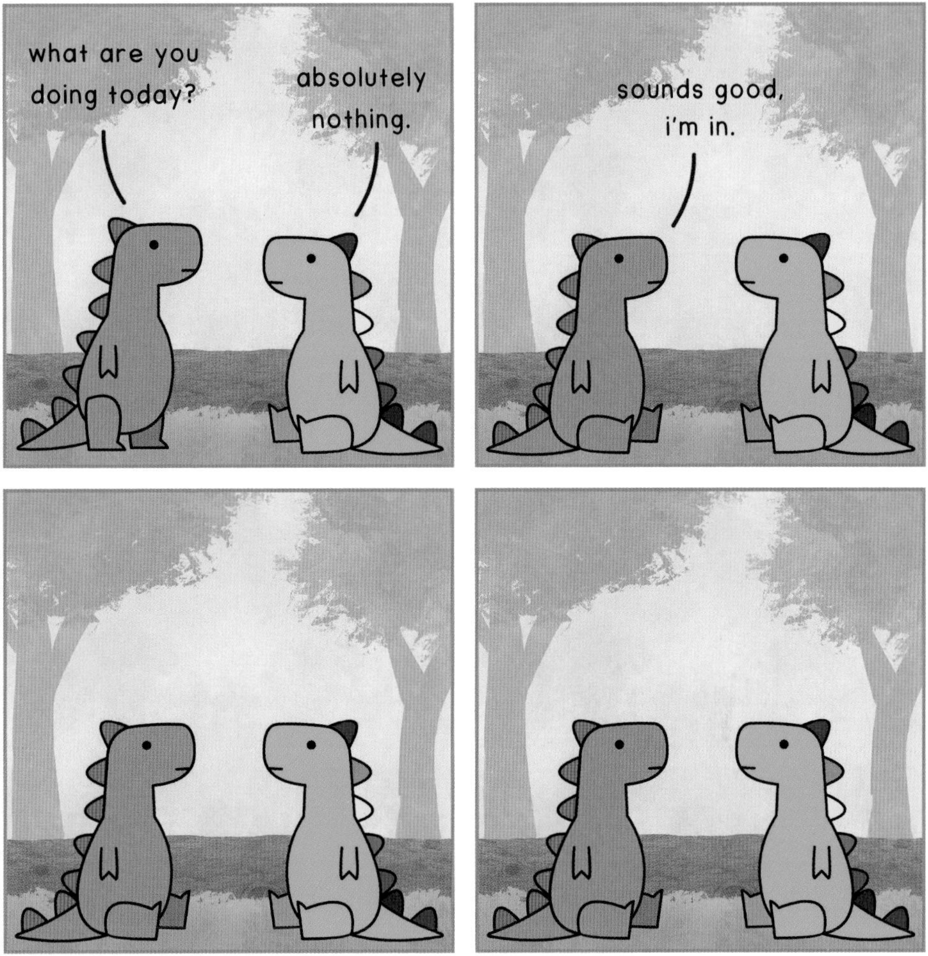
what are you doing today?
absolutely nothing.
sounds good, i'm in.

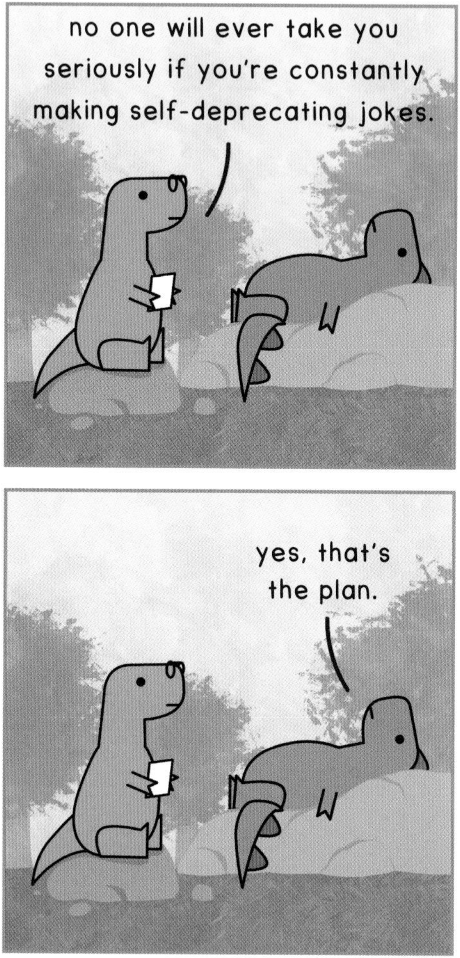
no one will ever take you seriously if you're constantly making self-deprecating jokes.
yes, that's the plan.

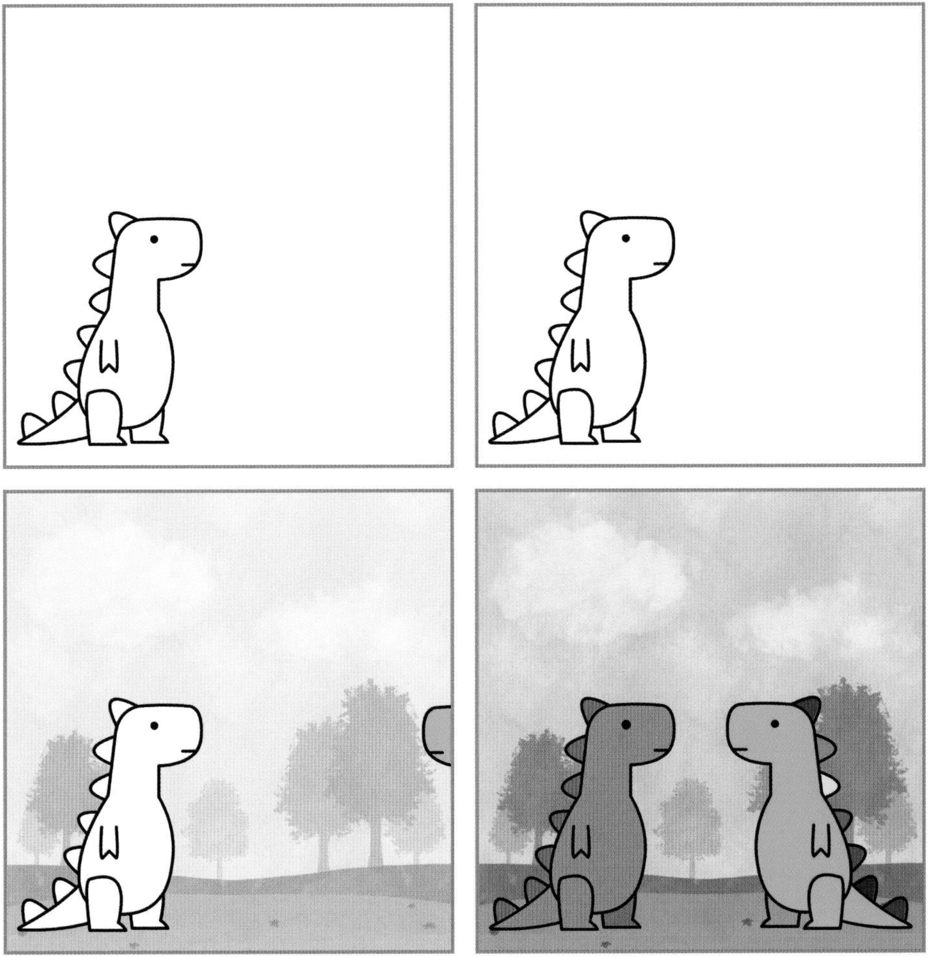

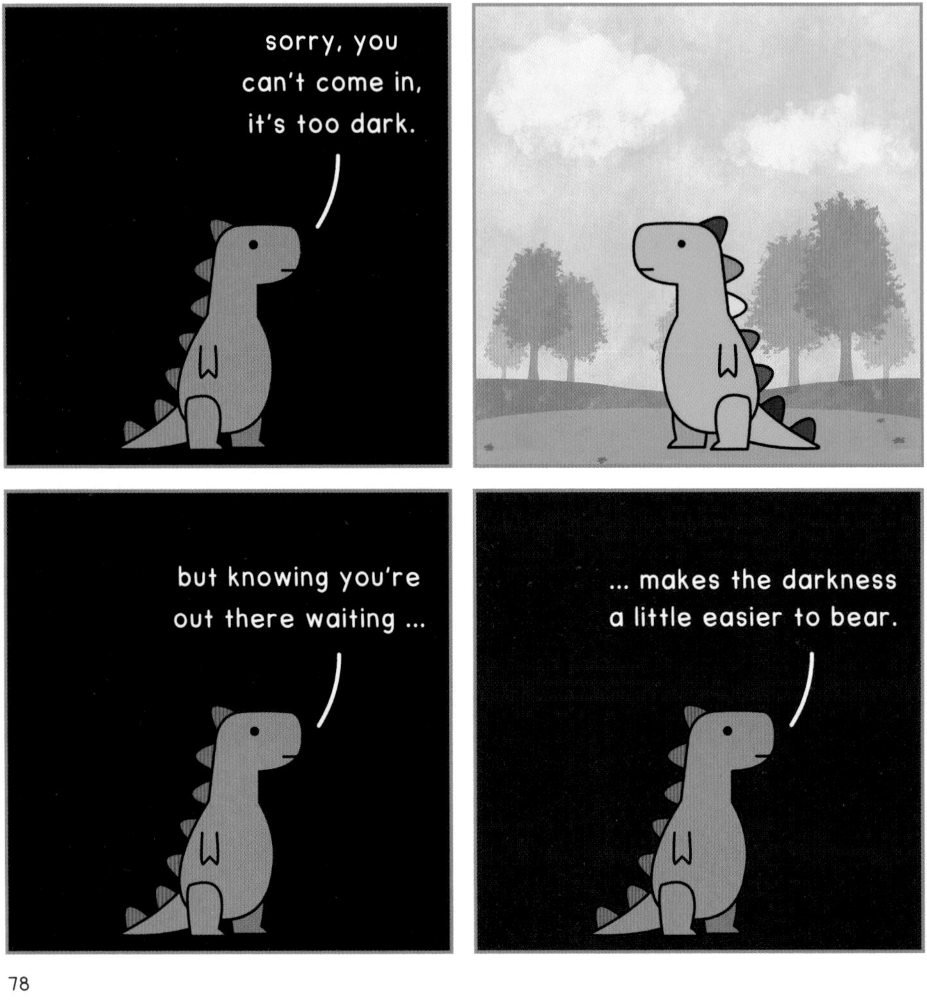
sorry, you can't come in, it's too dark.
but knowing you're out there waiting ...
... makes the darkness a little easier to bear.

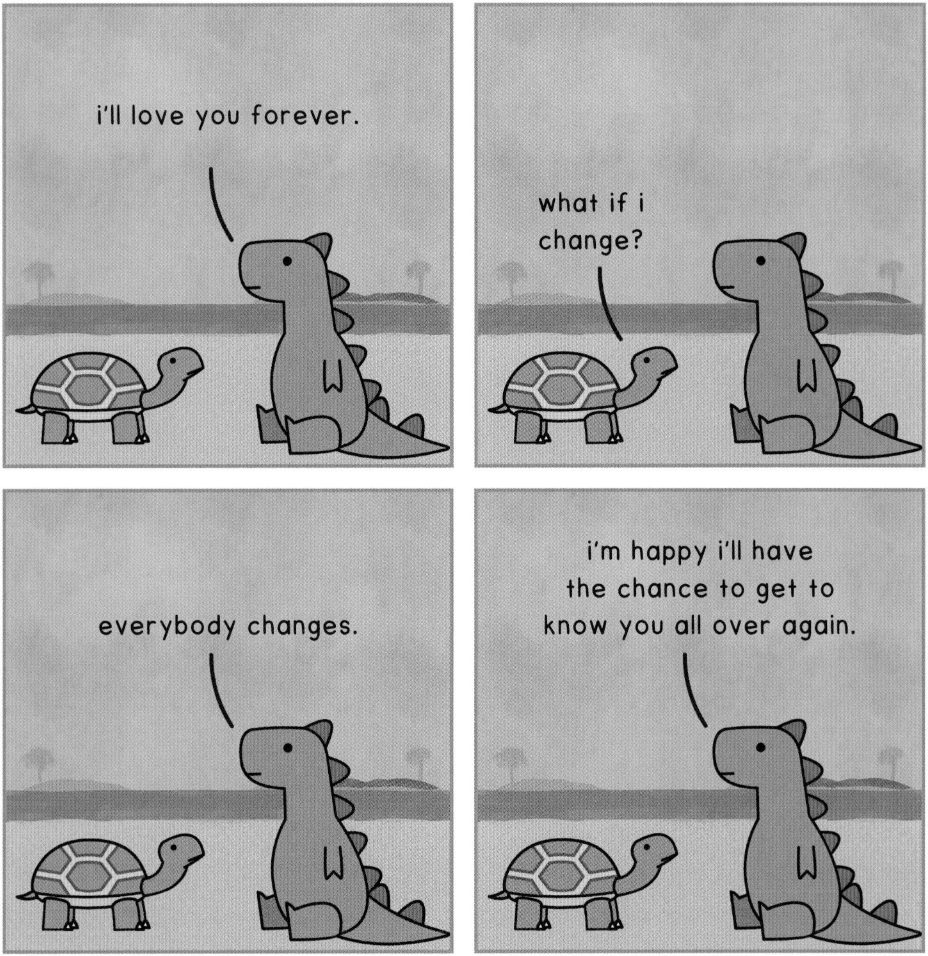
i'll love you forever.
what if i change?
everybody changes.
i'm happy i'll have the chance to get to know you all over again.

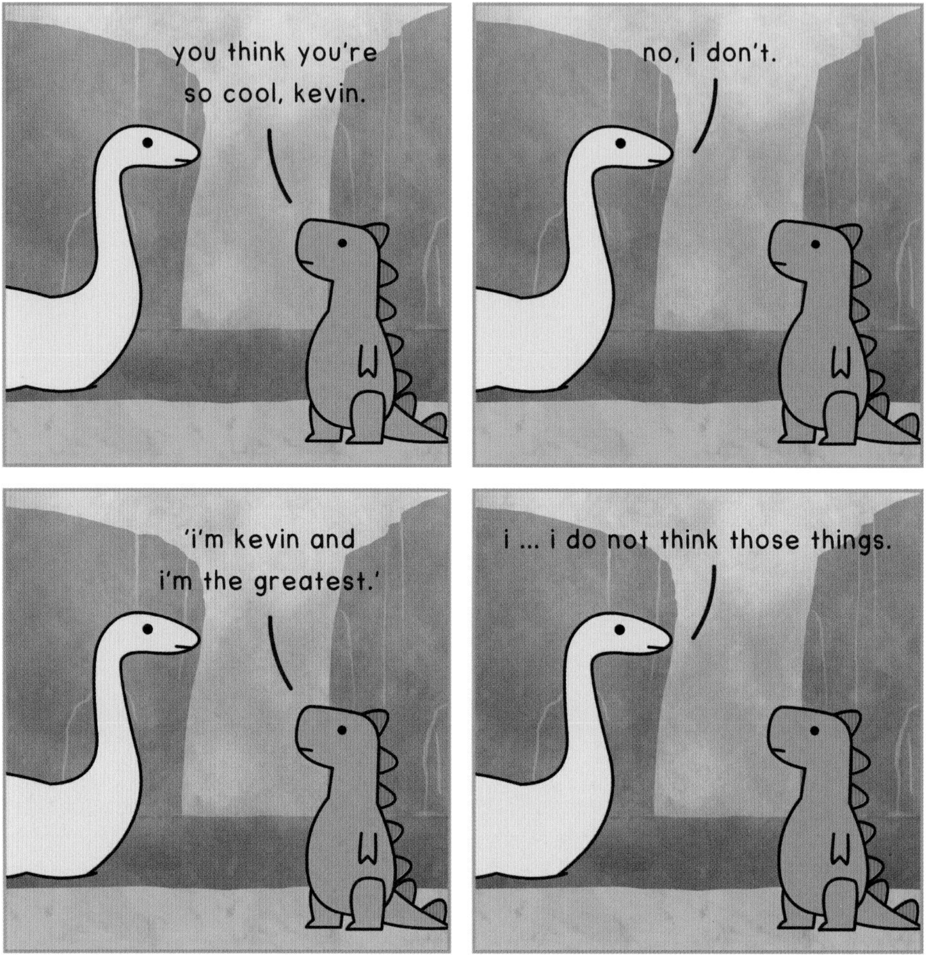
you think you're so cool, kevin.
no, i don't.
'i'm kevin and i'm the greatest.'
i ... i do not think those things.

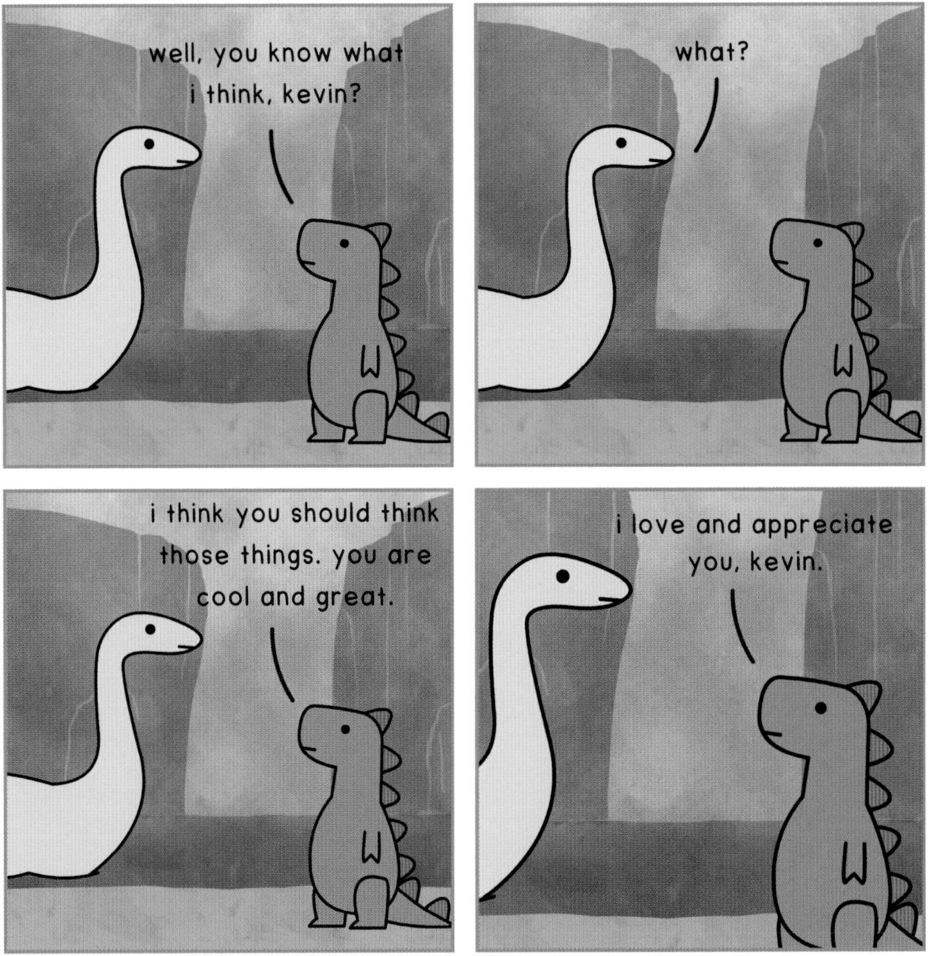
well, you know what i think, kevin?
what?
i think you should think those things. you are cool and great.
i love and appreciate you, kevin.

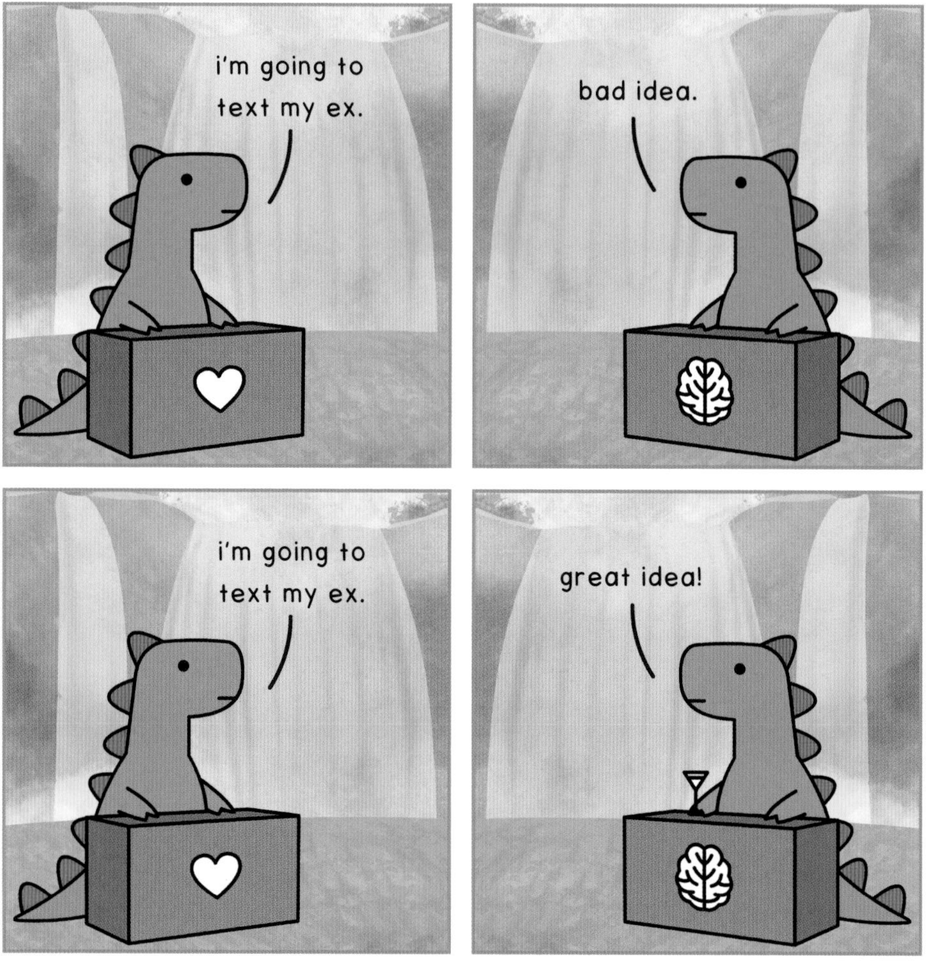
i'm going to text my ex.
bad idea.
i'm going to text my ex.
great idea!

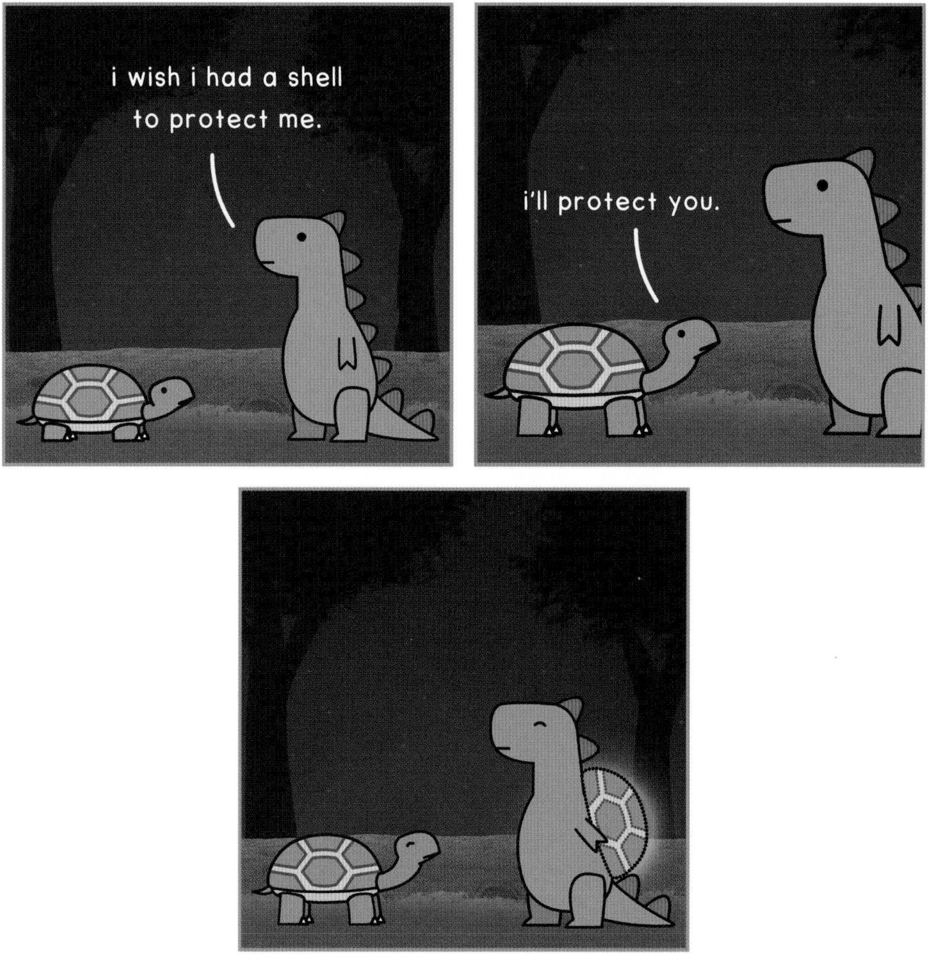
i wish i had a shell
to protect me.
i'll protect you.

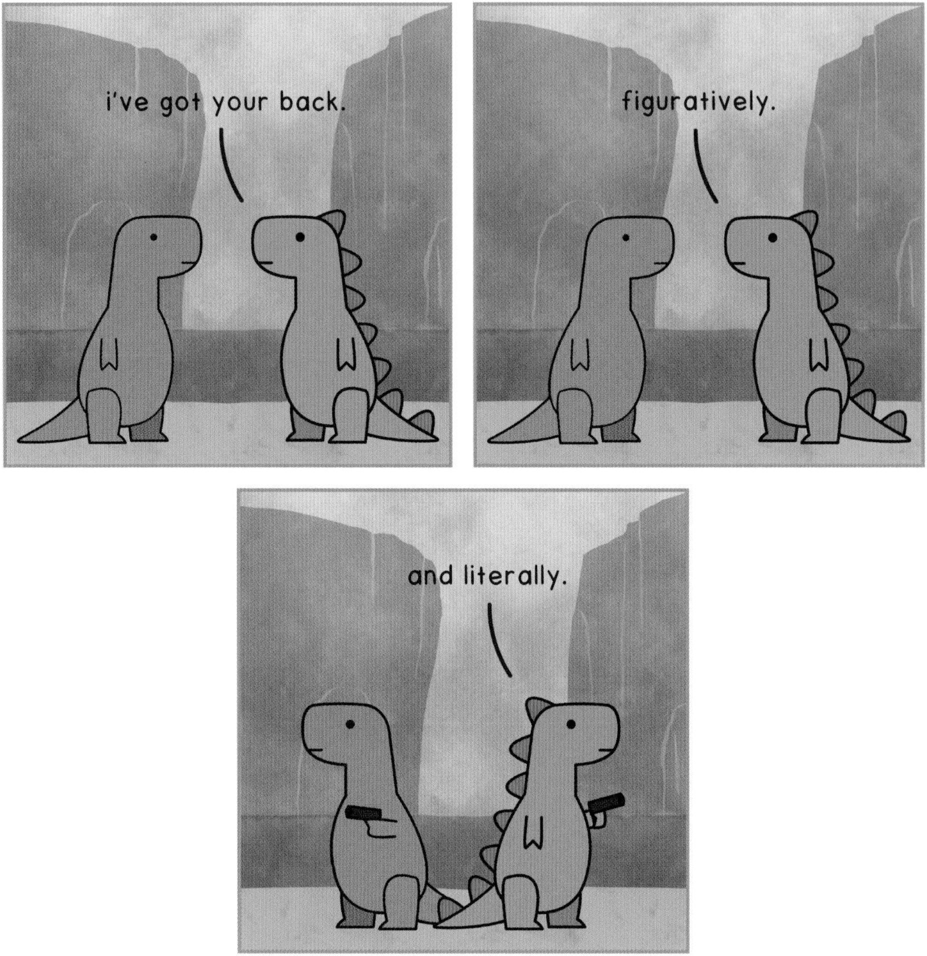
i've got your back.
figuratively.
and literally.

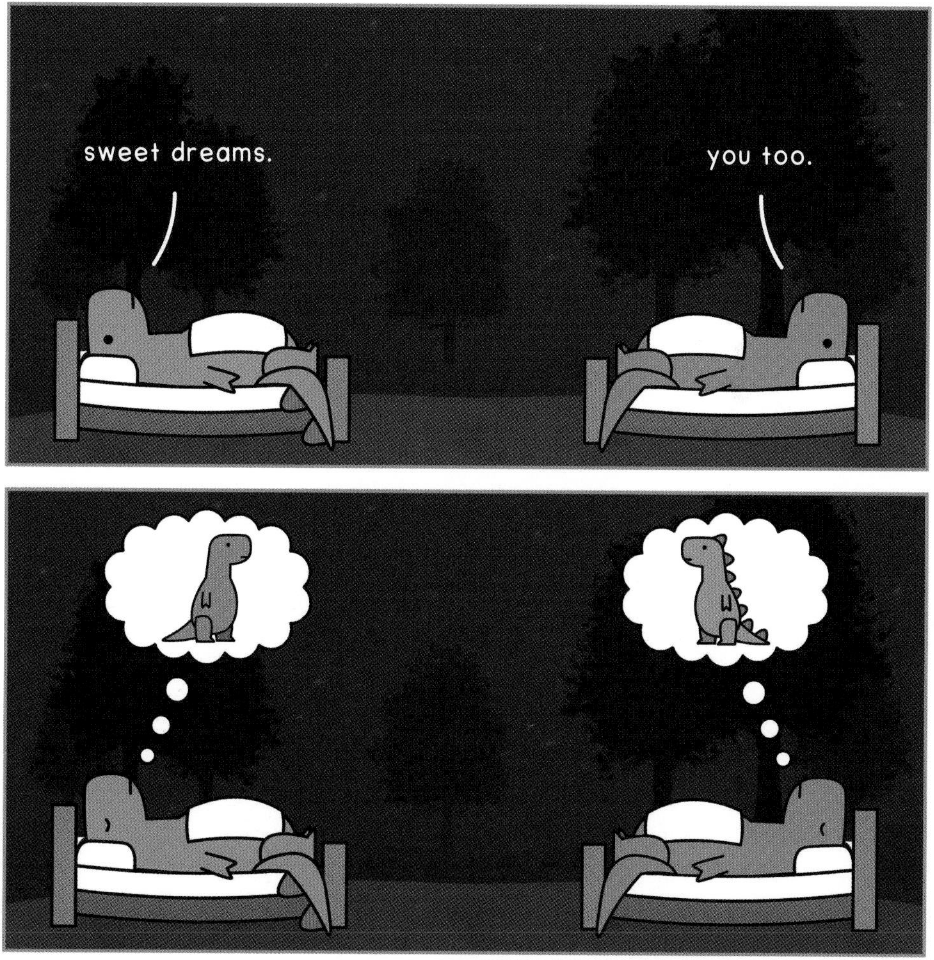
sweet dreams.
you too.

stress, overthinking, anxiety

the subtle art of thinking precisely the right amount

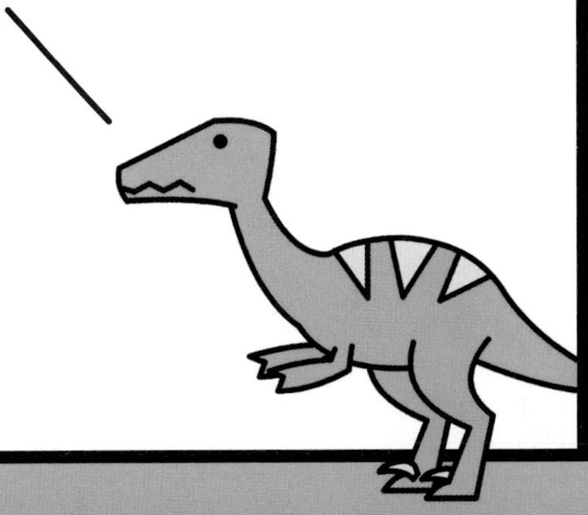

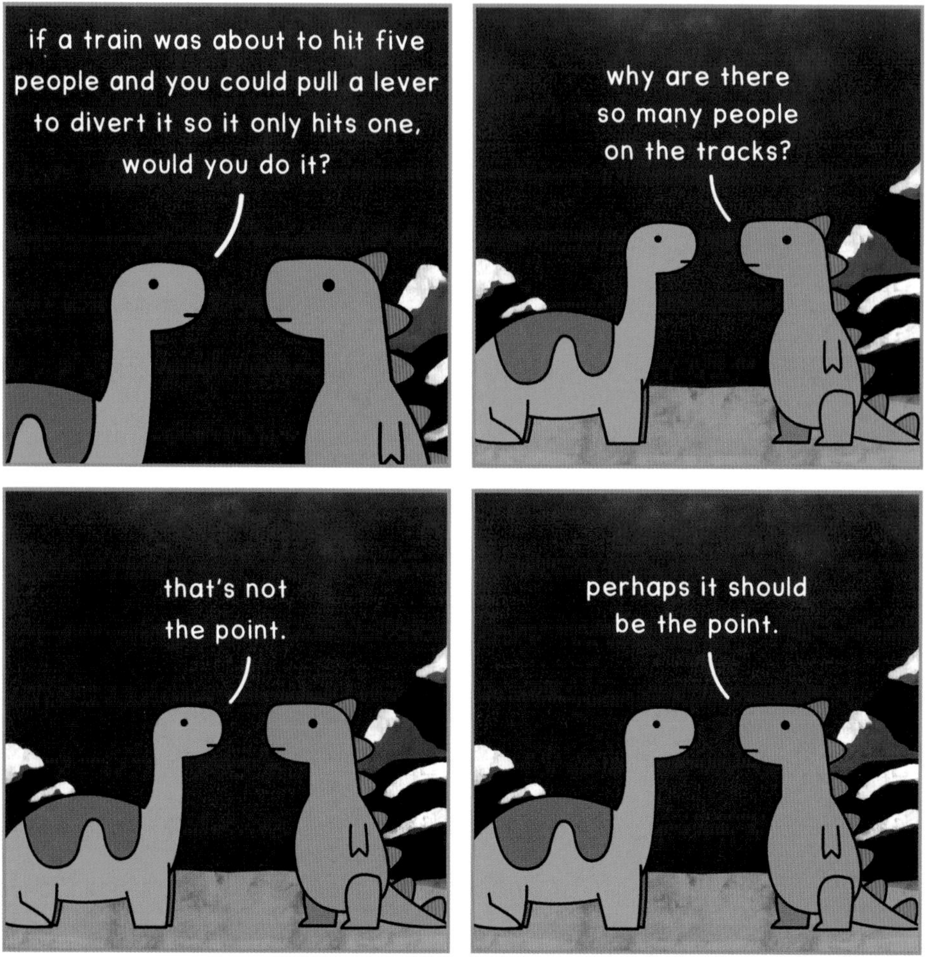
if a train was about to hit five people and you could pull a lever to divert it so it only hits one, would you do it?
why are there so many people on the tracks?
that's not the point.
perhaps it should be the point.

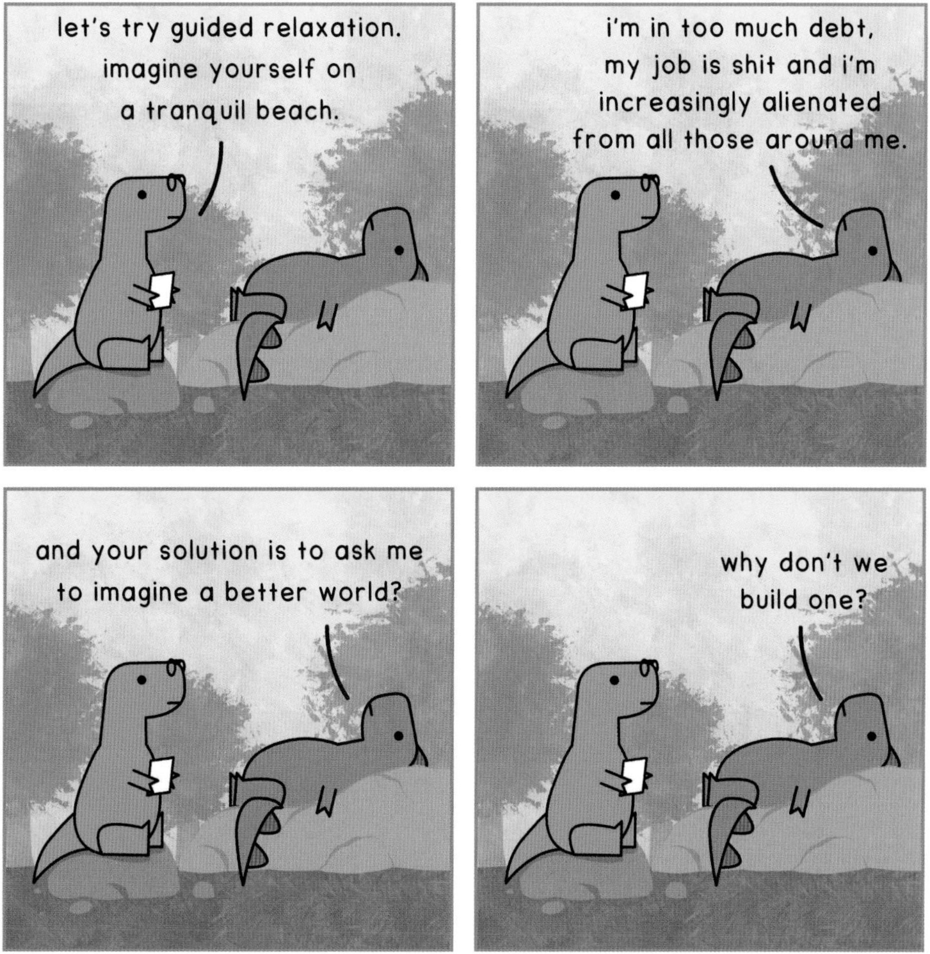
let's try guided relaxation. imagine yourself on a tranquil beach.
i'm in too much debt, my job is shit and i'm increasingly alienated from all those around me.
and your solution is to ask me to imagine a better world?
why don't we build one?

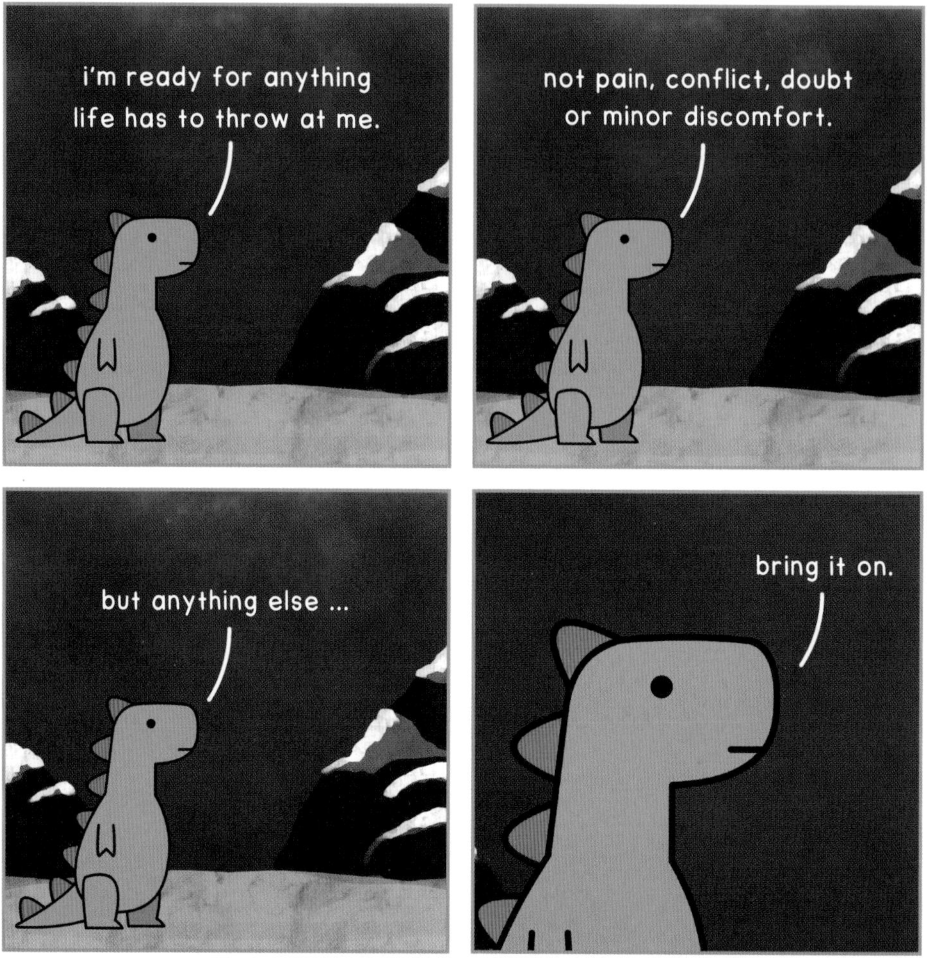
i'm ready for anything life has to throw at me.
not pain, conflict, doubt or minor discomfort.
but anything else ...
bring it on.

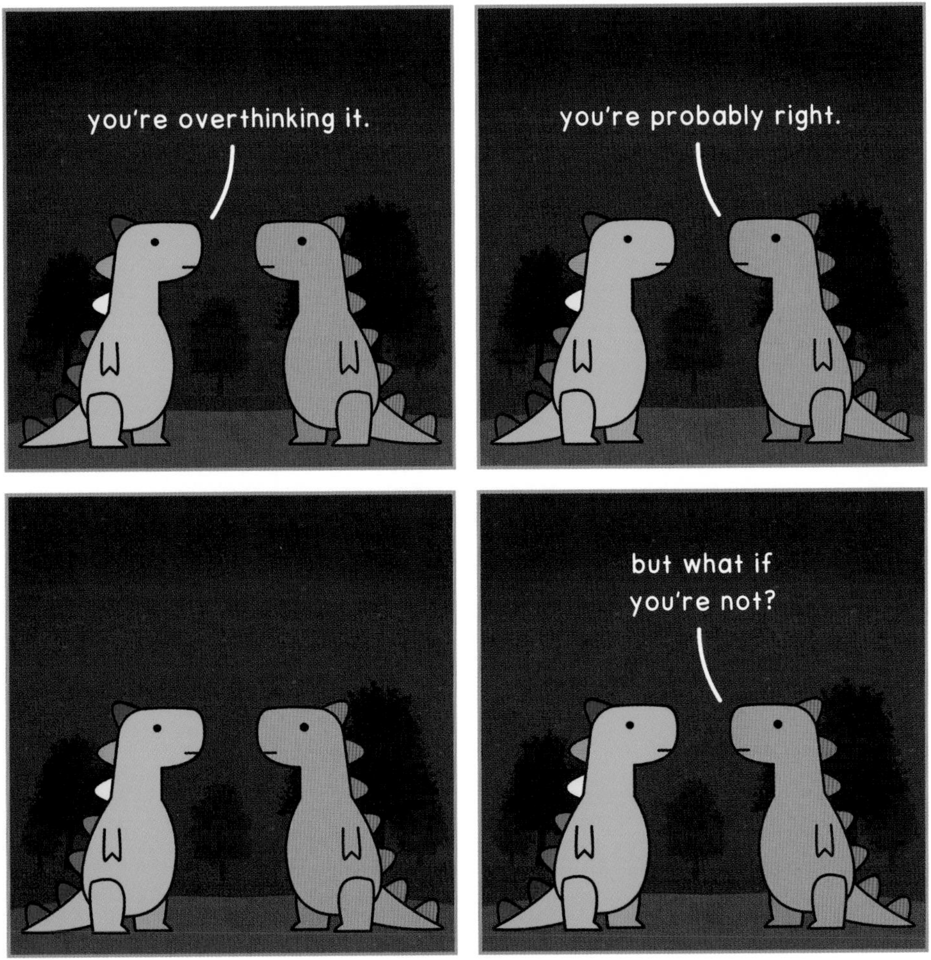
you're overthinking it.
you're probably right.
but what if you're not?

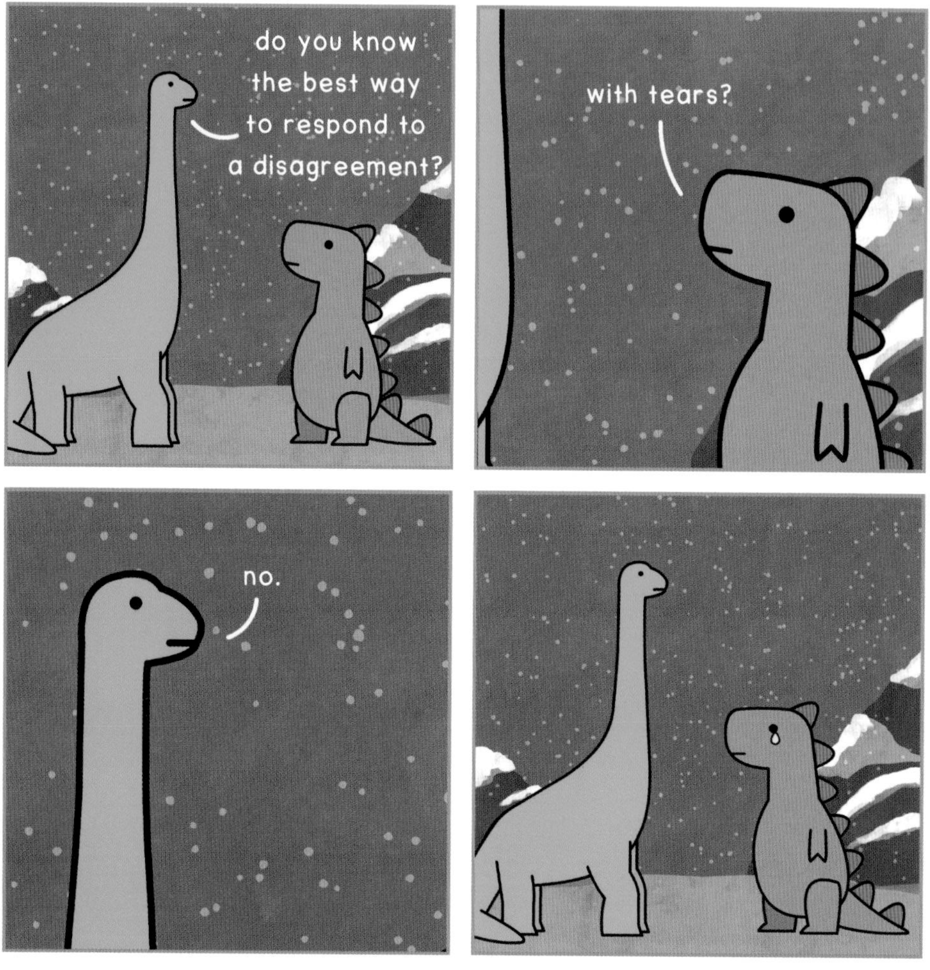
do you know the best way to respond to a disagreement?
with tears?
no.

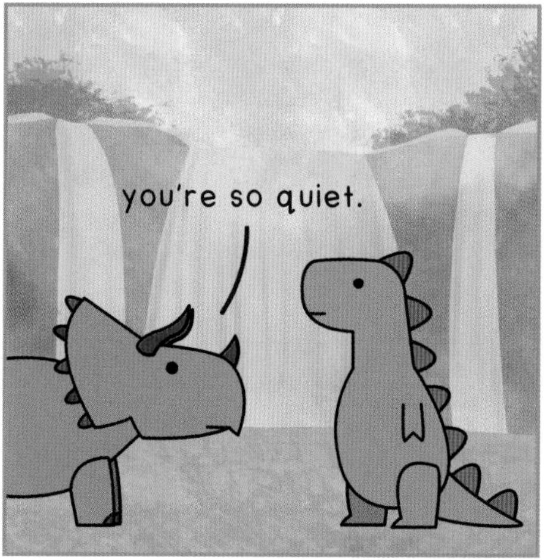
you're so quiet.

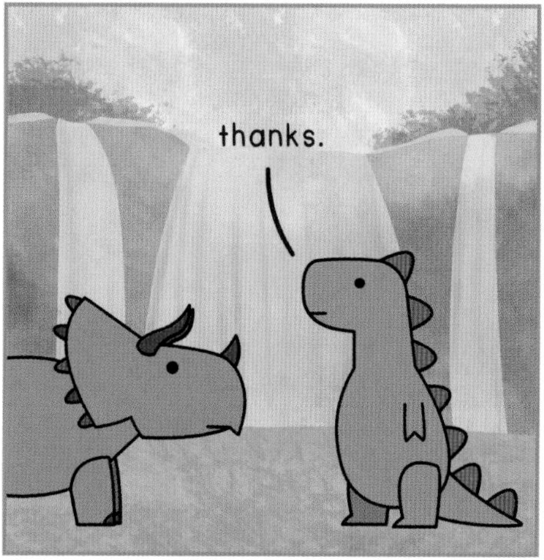
thanks.

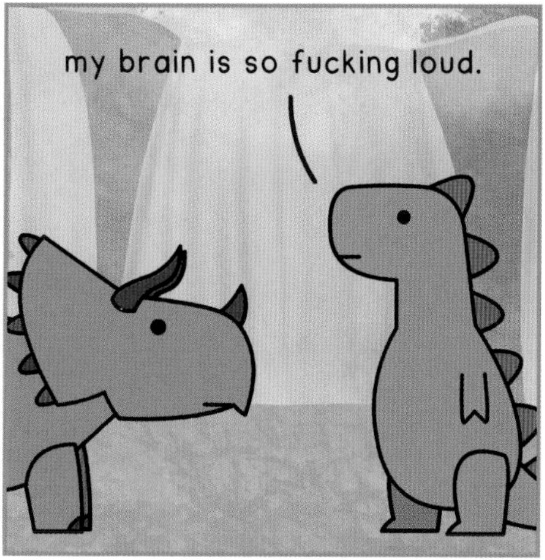
my brain is so fucking loud.

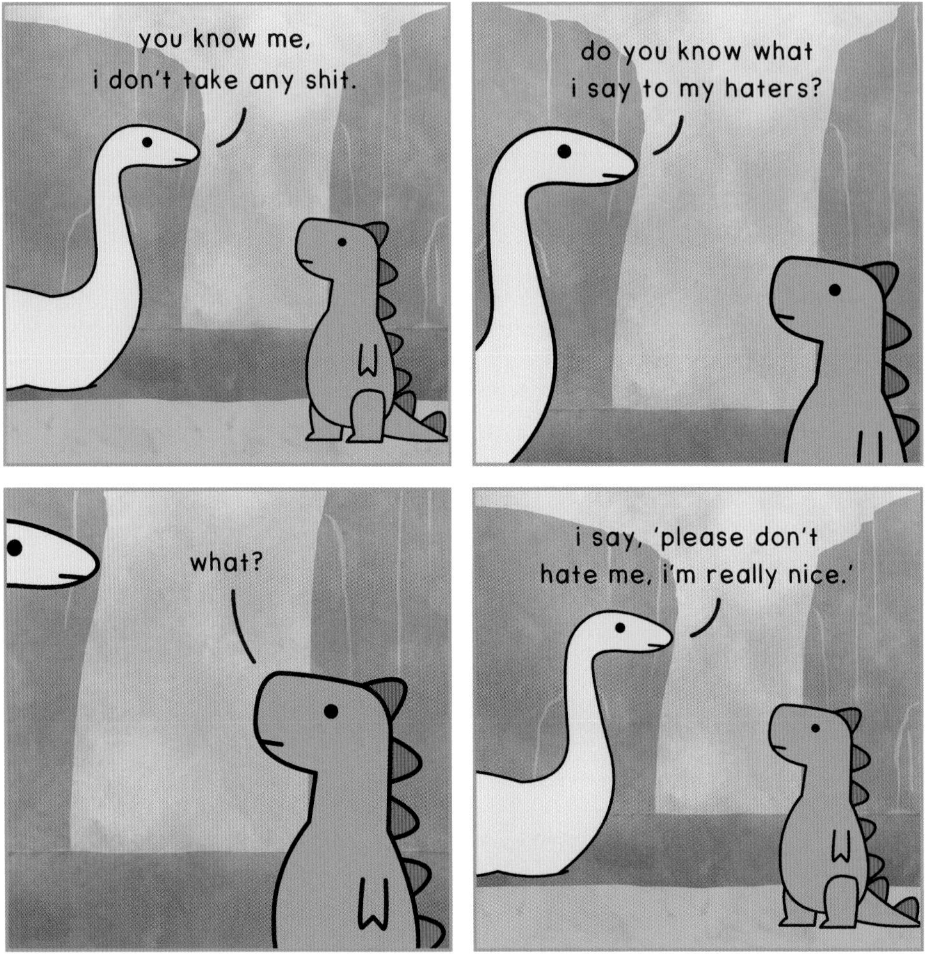
you know me,
i don't take any shit.
do you know what
i say to my haters?
what?
i say, 'please don't
hate me, i'm really nice.'

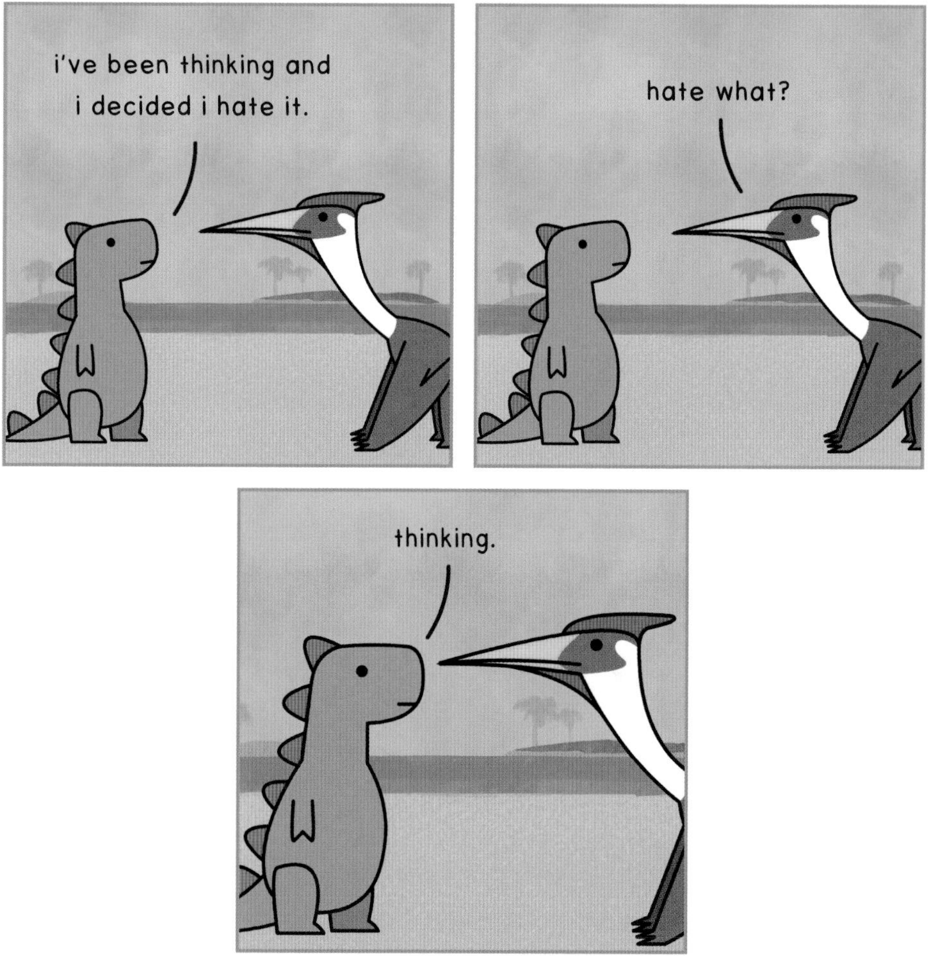
i've been thinking and i decided i hate it.
hate what?
thinking.

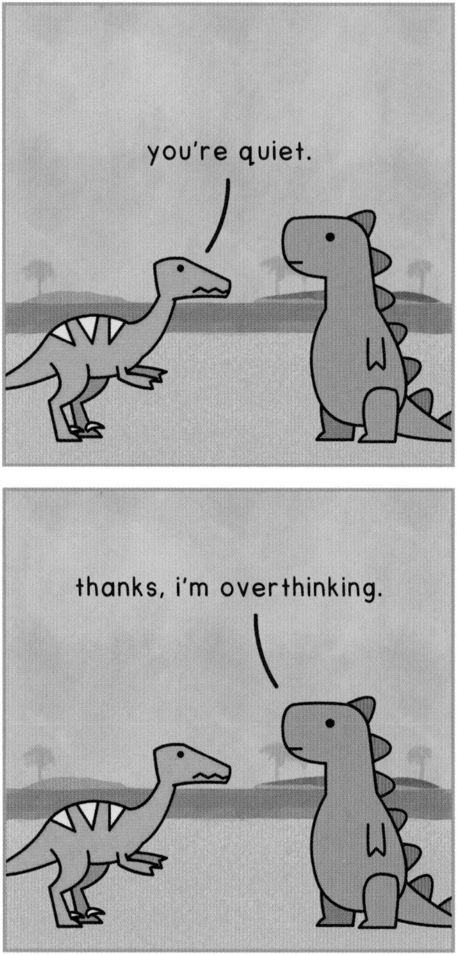
you're quiet.
thanks, i'm overthinking.

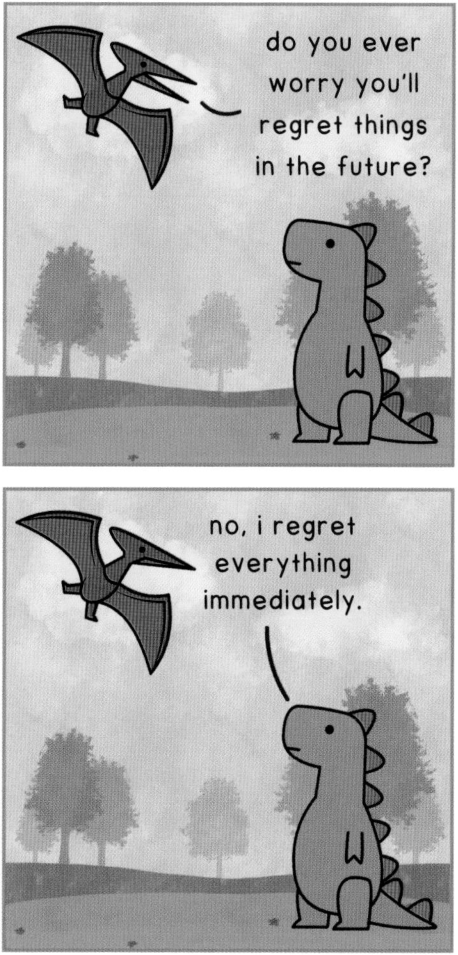
do you ever worry you'll regret things in the future?
no, i regret everything immediately.

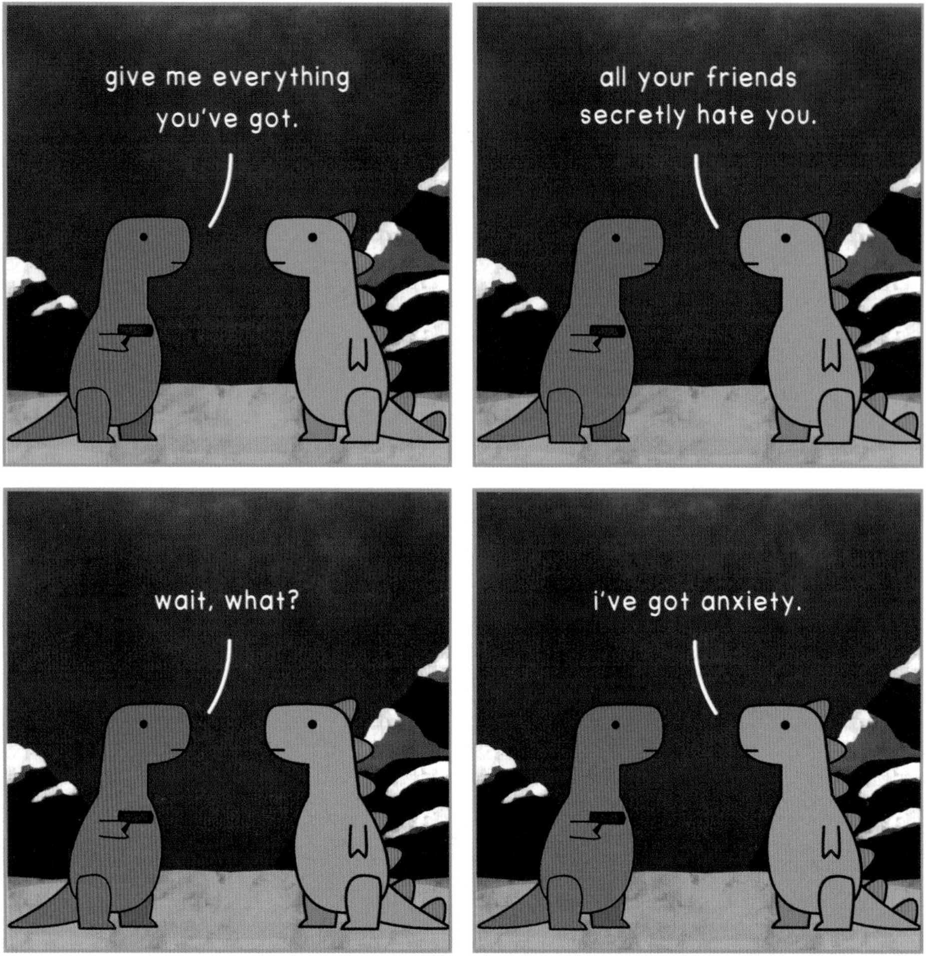
give me everything you've got.
all your friends secretly hate you.
wait, what?
i've got anxiety.

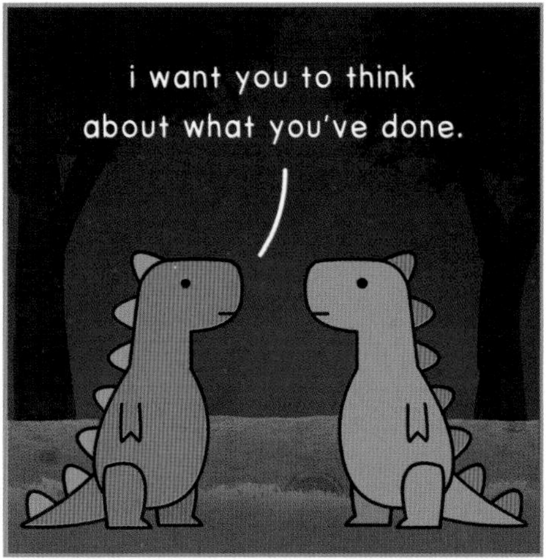
i want you to think
about what you've done.

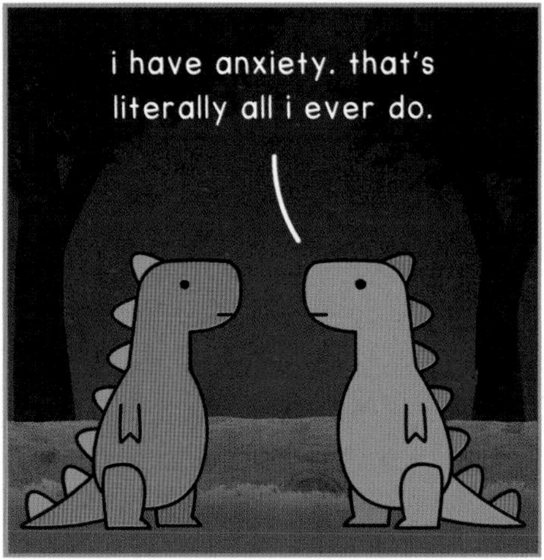
i have anxiety. that's
literally all i ever do.

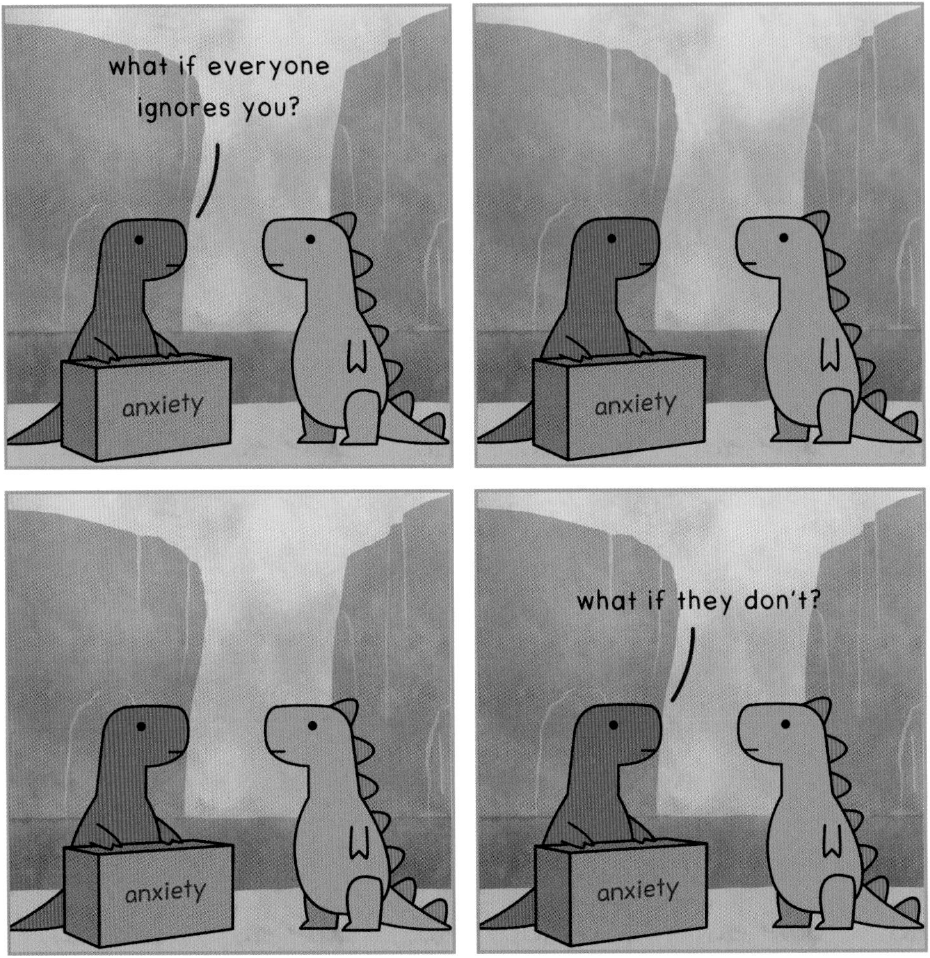
what if everyone ignores you?
anxiety
anxiety
anxiety
what if they don't?
anxiety

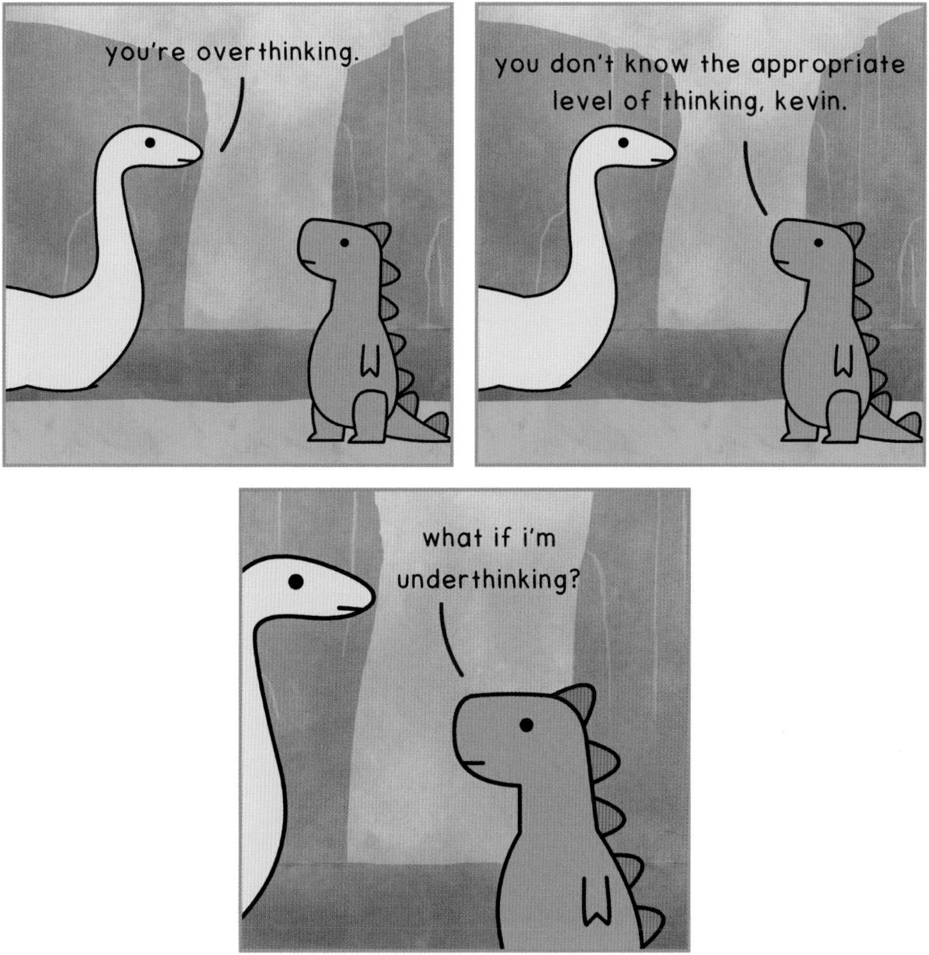
you're overthinking.
you don't know the appropriate level of thinking, kevin.
what if i'm underthinking?

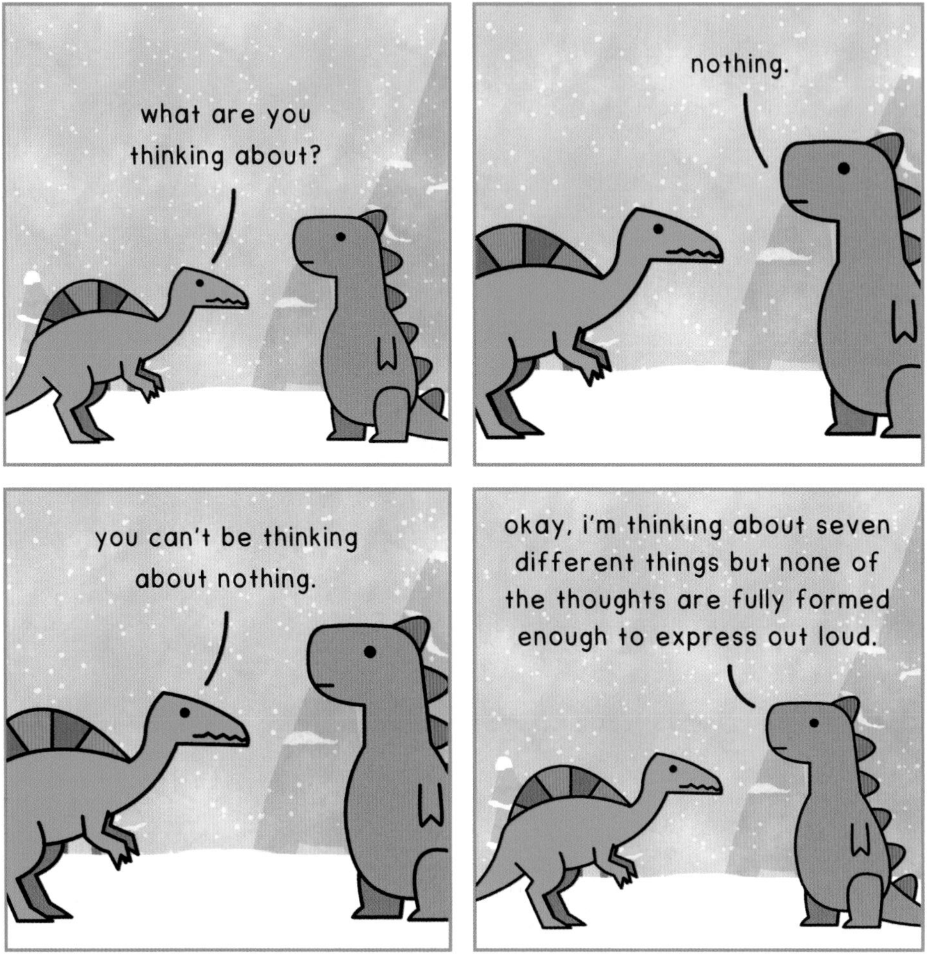
what are you thinking about?
nothing.
you can't be thinking about nothing.
okay, i'm thinking about seven different things but none of the thoughts are fully formed enough to express out loud.

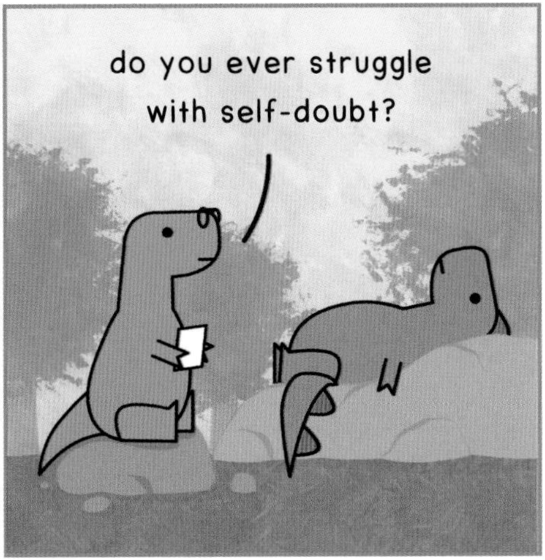
do you ever struggle
with self-doubt?

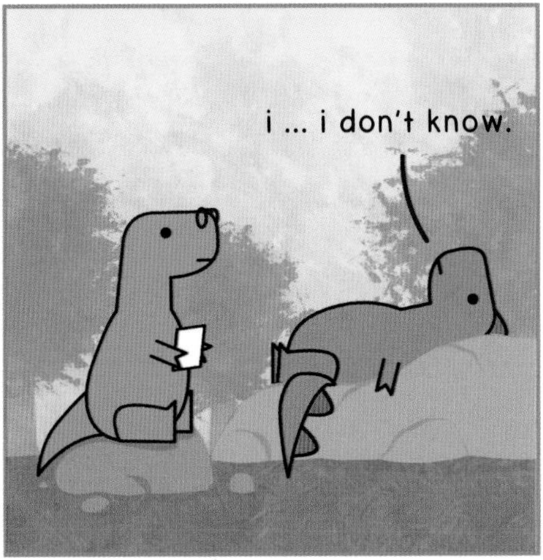
i ... i don't know.

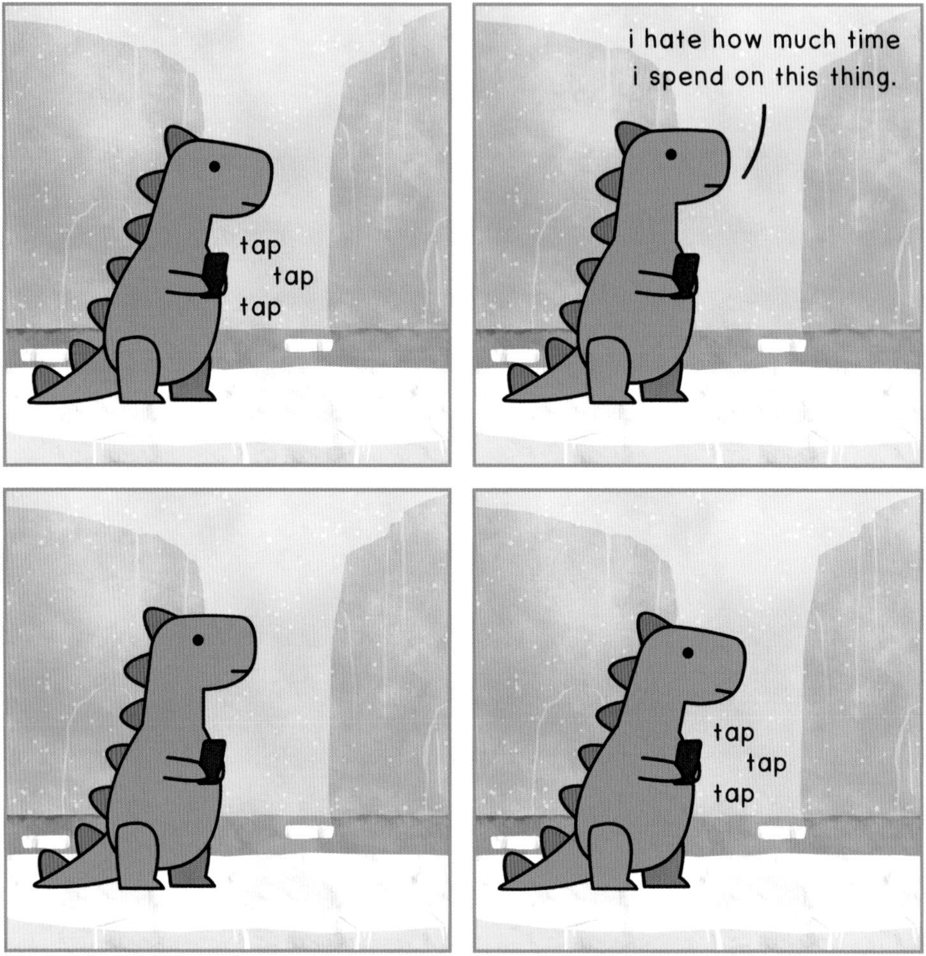
tap
tap
tap
i hate how much time i spend on this thing.
tap
tap
tap

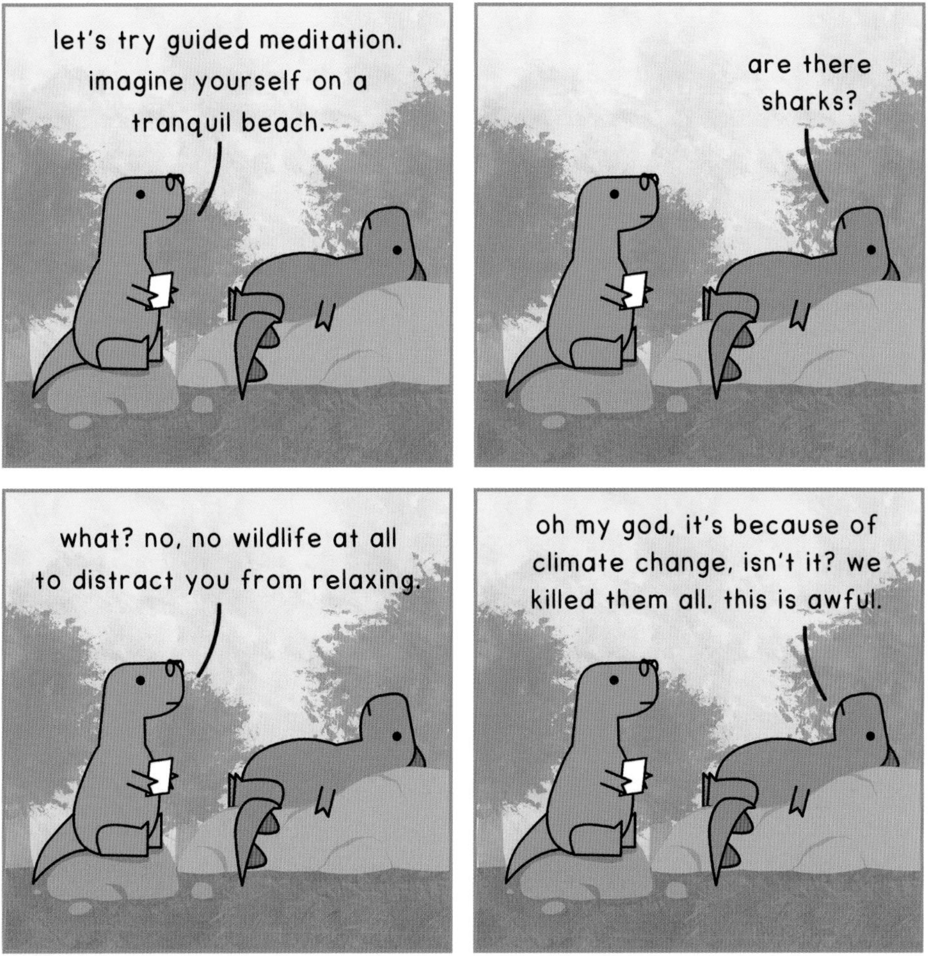
let's try guided meditation. imagine yourself on a tranquil beach.
are there sharks?
what? no, no wildlife at all to distract you from relaxing.
oh my god, it's because of climate change, isn't it? we killed them all. this is awful.

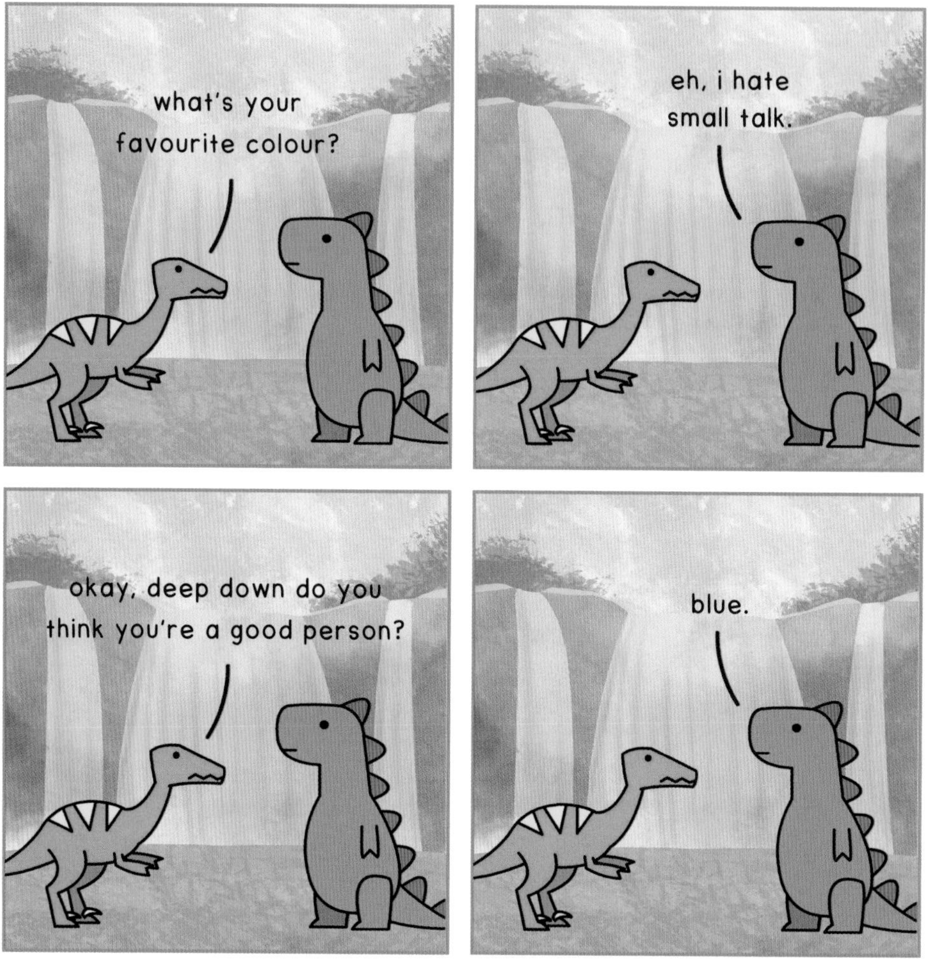
what's your favourite colour?
eh, i hate small talk.
okay, deep down do you think you're a good person?
blue.

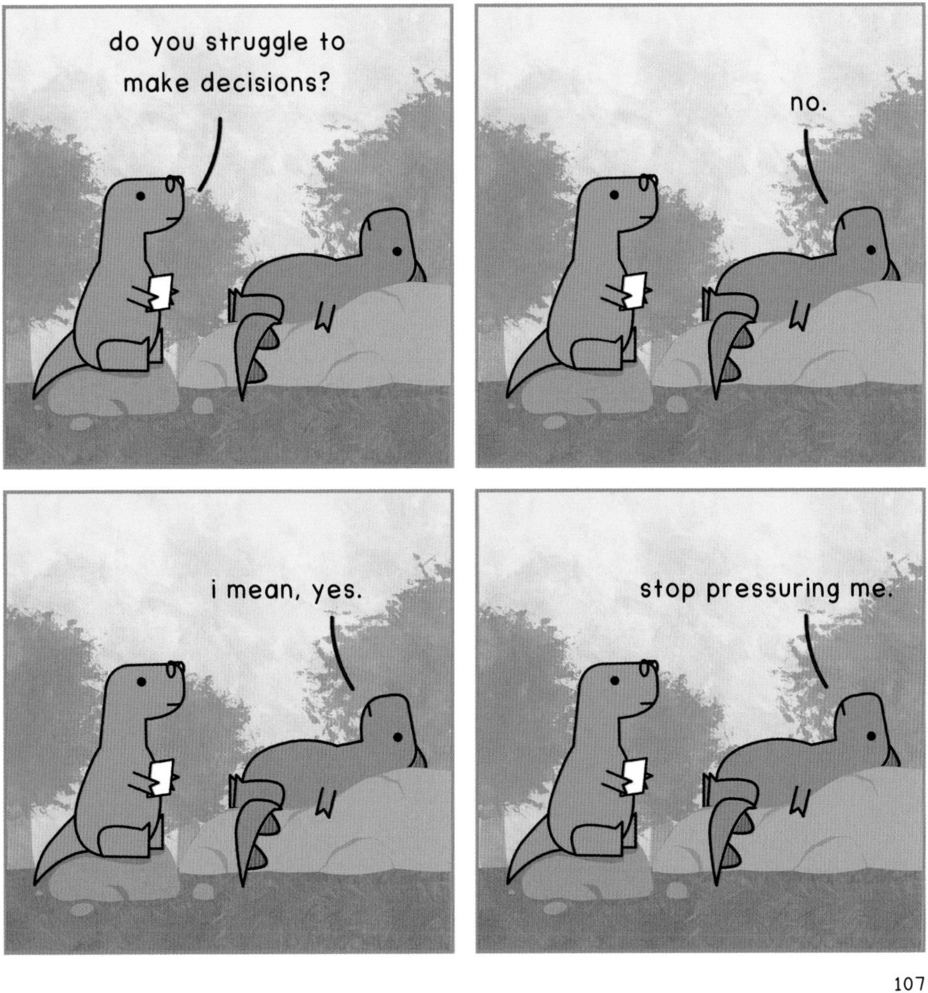
do you struggle to make decisions?
no.
i mean, yes.
stop pressuring me.

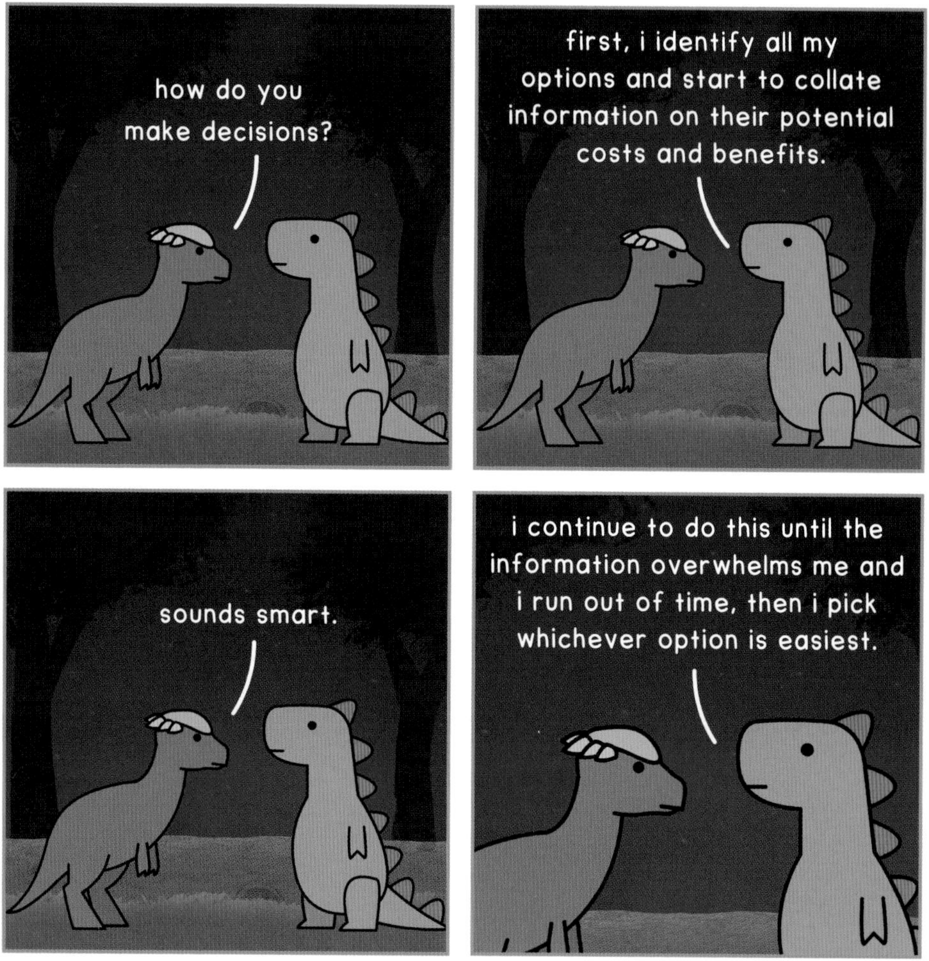
how do you
make decisions?
first, i identify all my
options and start to collate
information on their potential
costs and benefits.
sounds smart.
i continue to do this until the
information overwhelms me and
i run out of time, then i pick
whichever option is easiest.

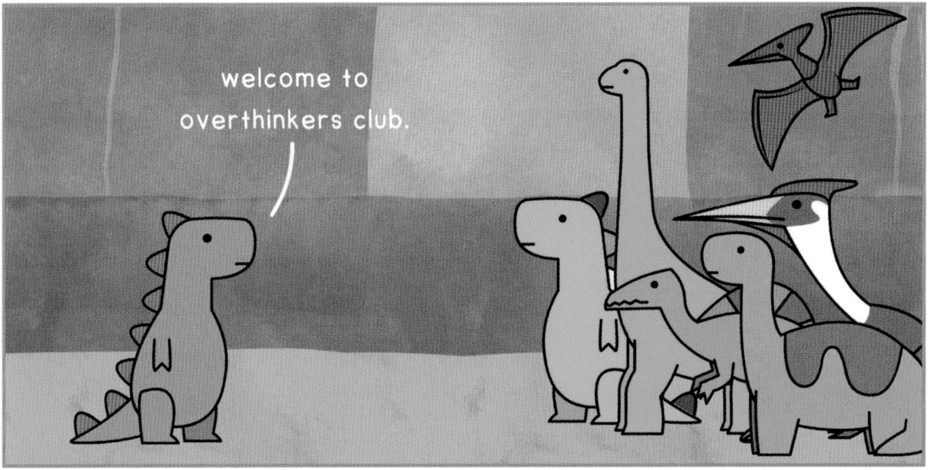
welcome to overthinkers club.

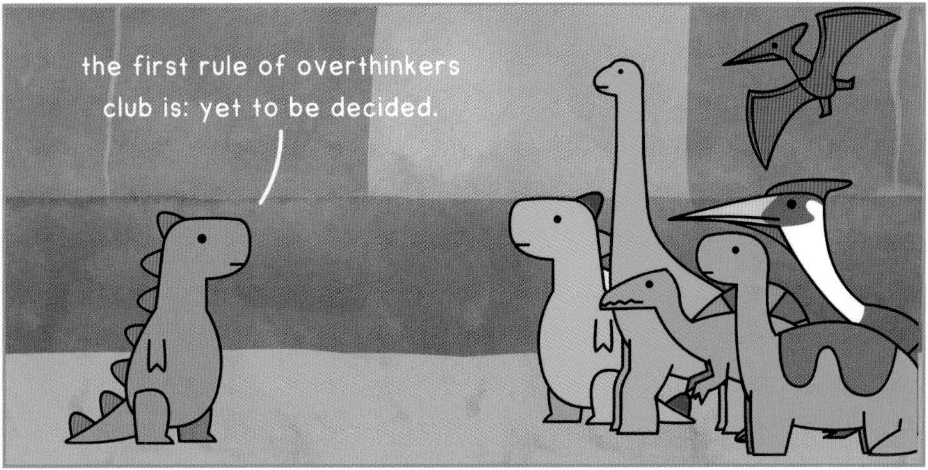
the first rule of overthinkers club is: yet to be decided.

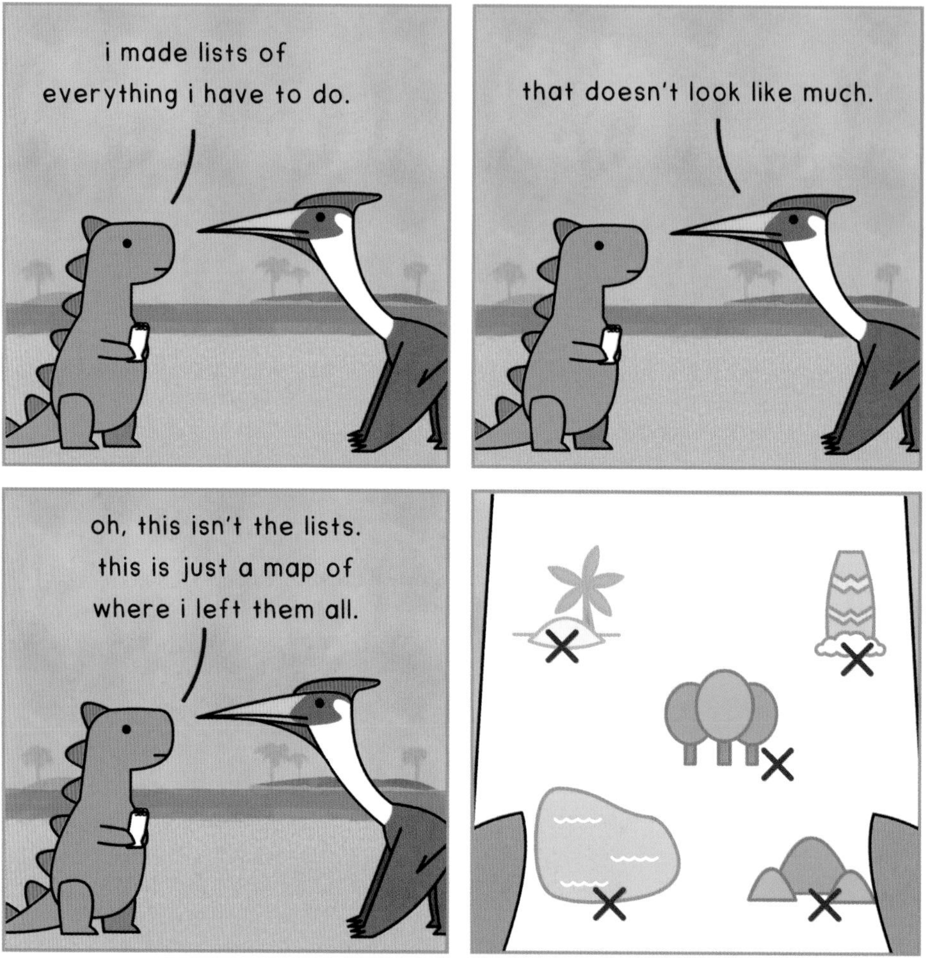
i made lists of
everything i have to do.
that doesn't look like much.
oh, this isn't the lists.
this is just a map of
where i left them all.

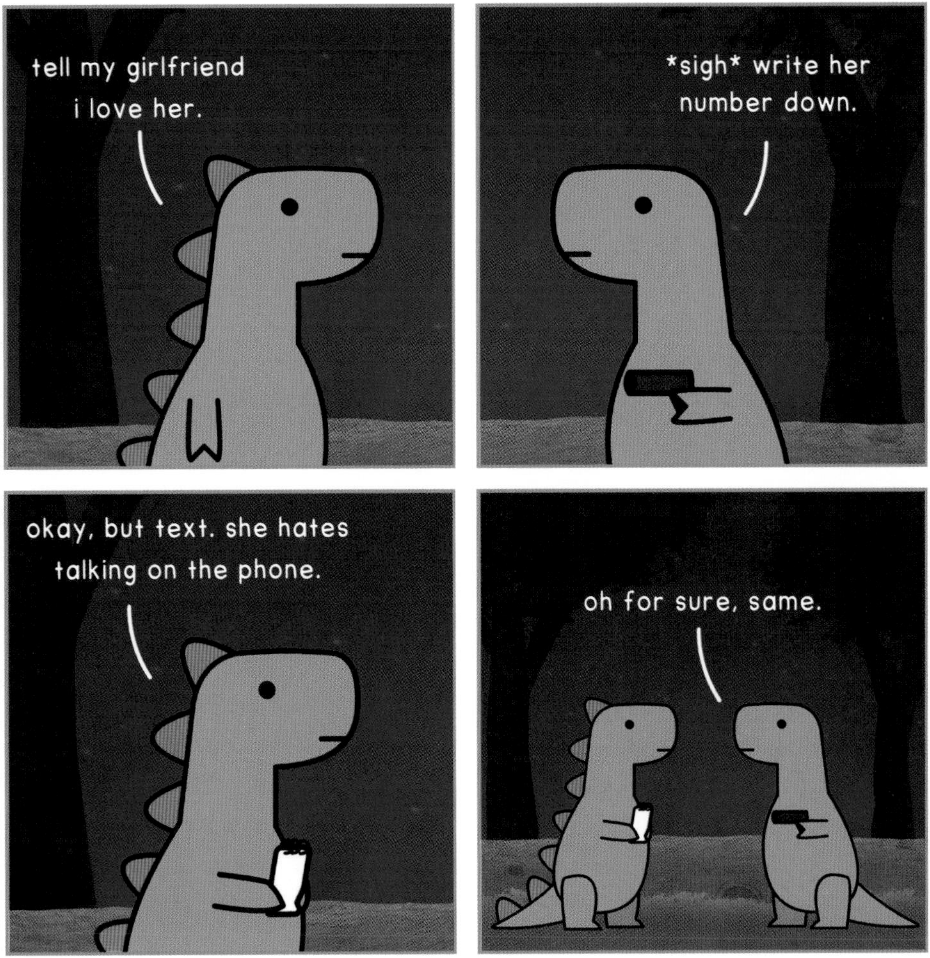
tell my girlfriend i love her.
sigh write her number down.
okay, but text. she hates talking on the phone.
oh for sure, same.

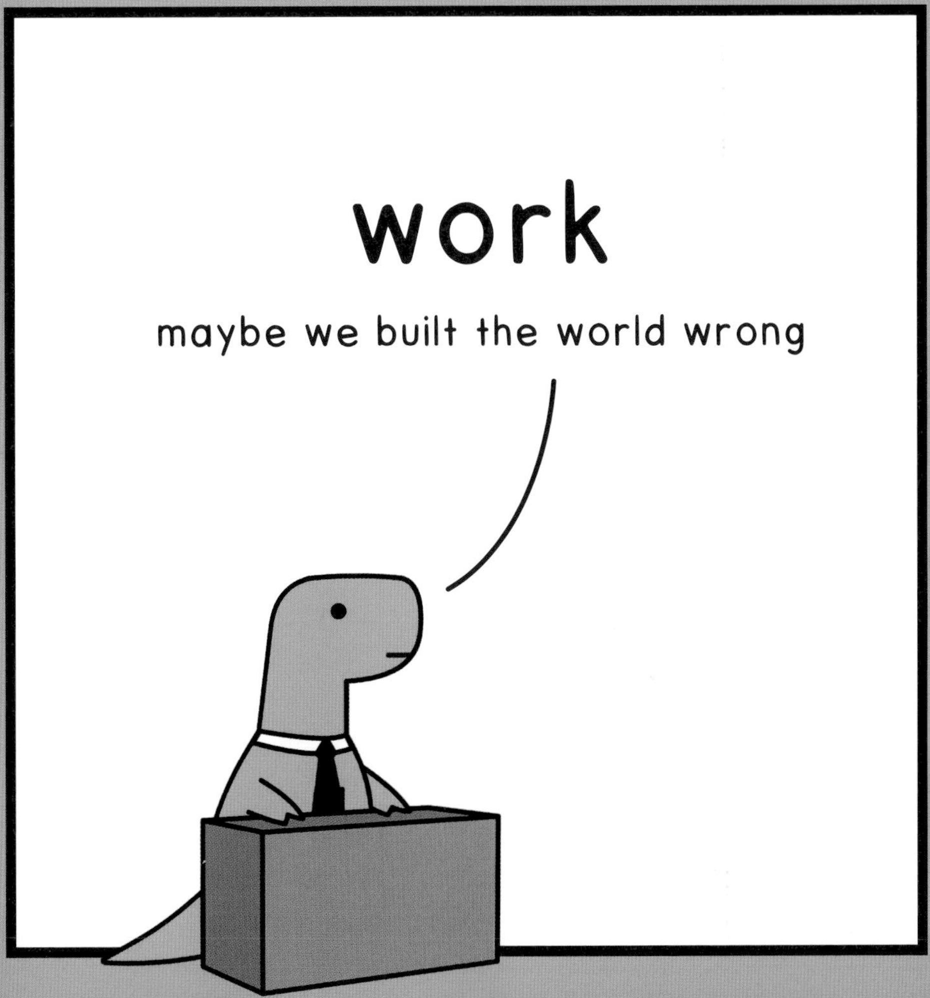
work
maybe we built the world wrong

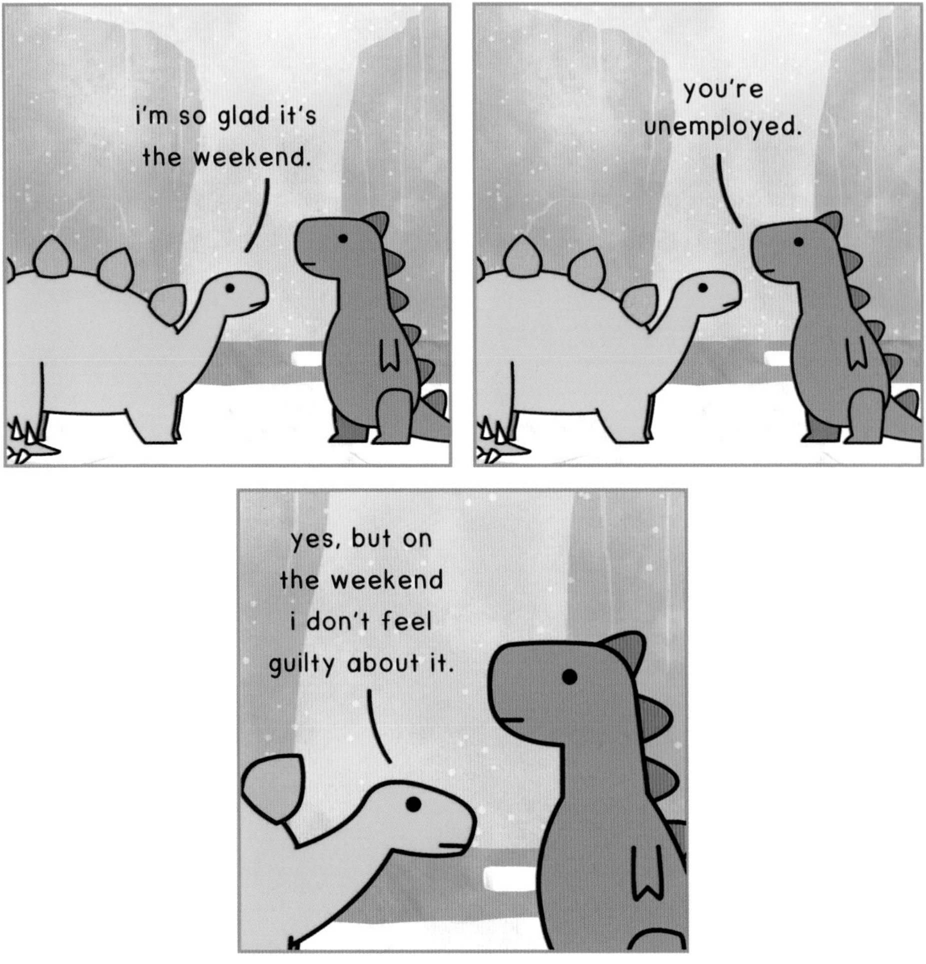
i'm so glad it's the weekend.
you're unemployed.
yes, but on the weekend i don't feel guilty about it.

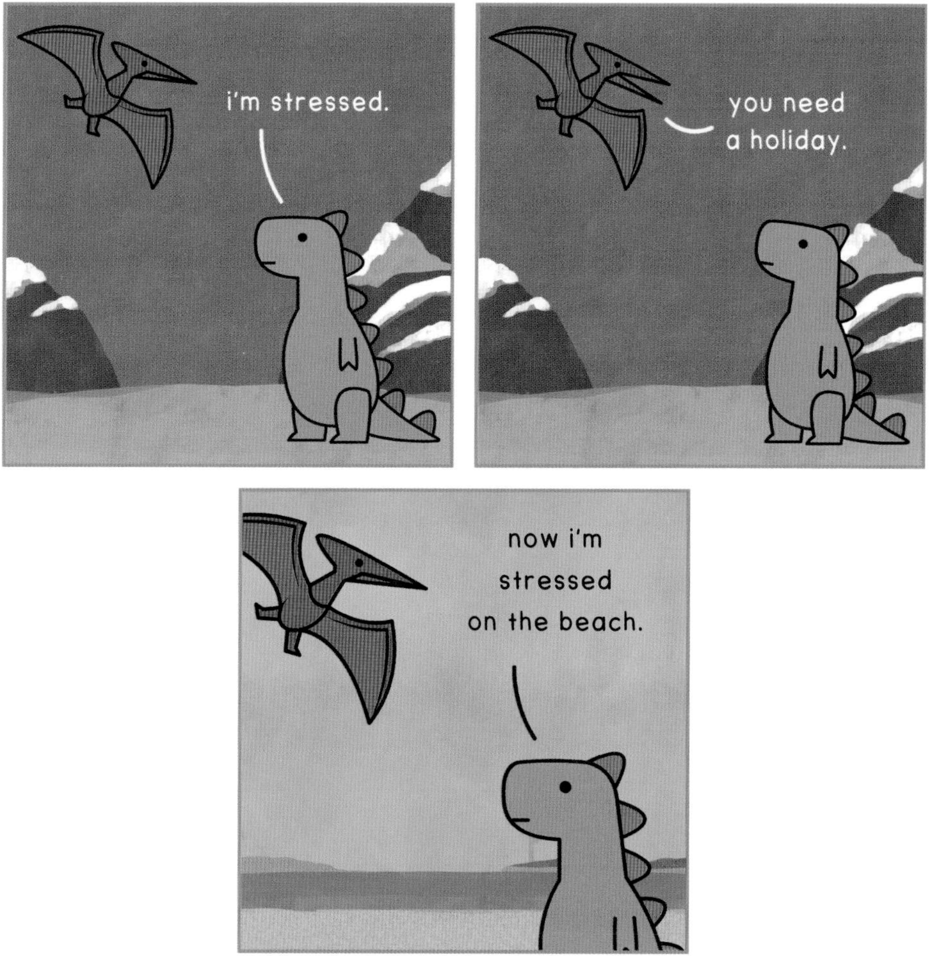
i'm stressed.
you need a holiday.
now i'm stressed on the beach.

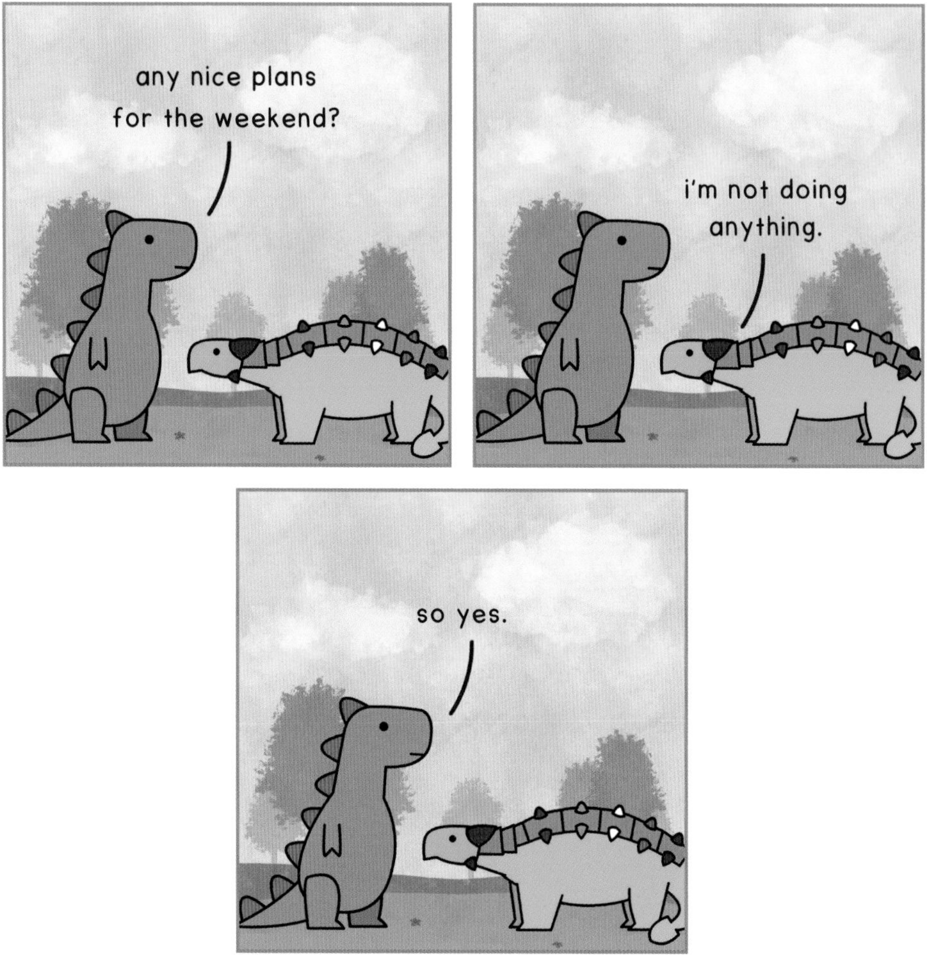
any nice plans for the weekend?
i'm not doing anything.
so yes.

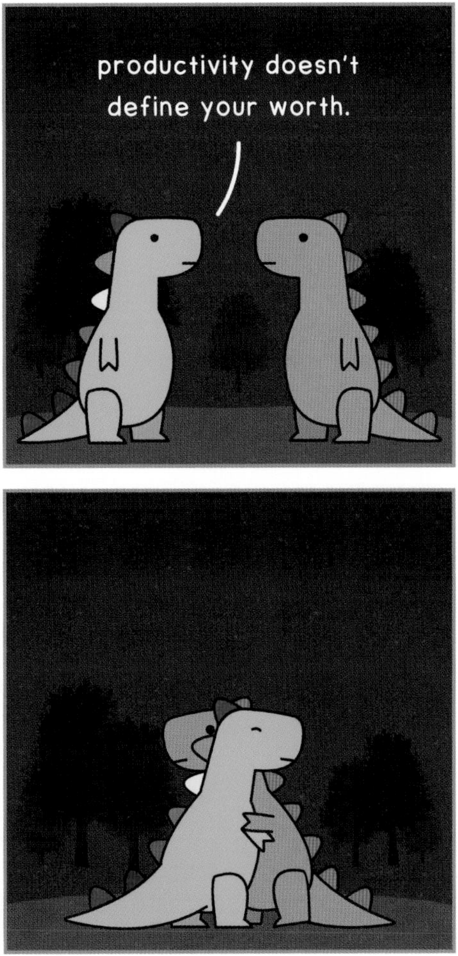
productivity doesn't define your worth.

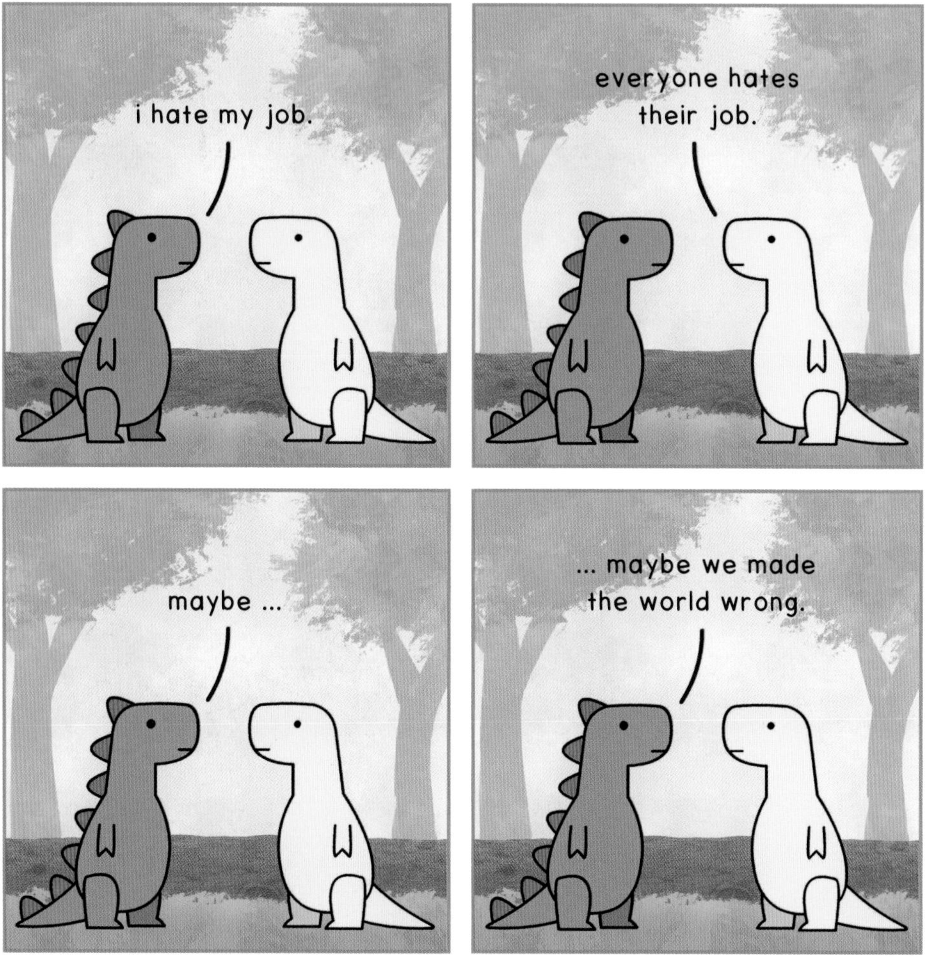
i hate my job.
everyone hates their job.
maybe ...
... maybe we made the world wrong.

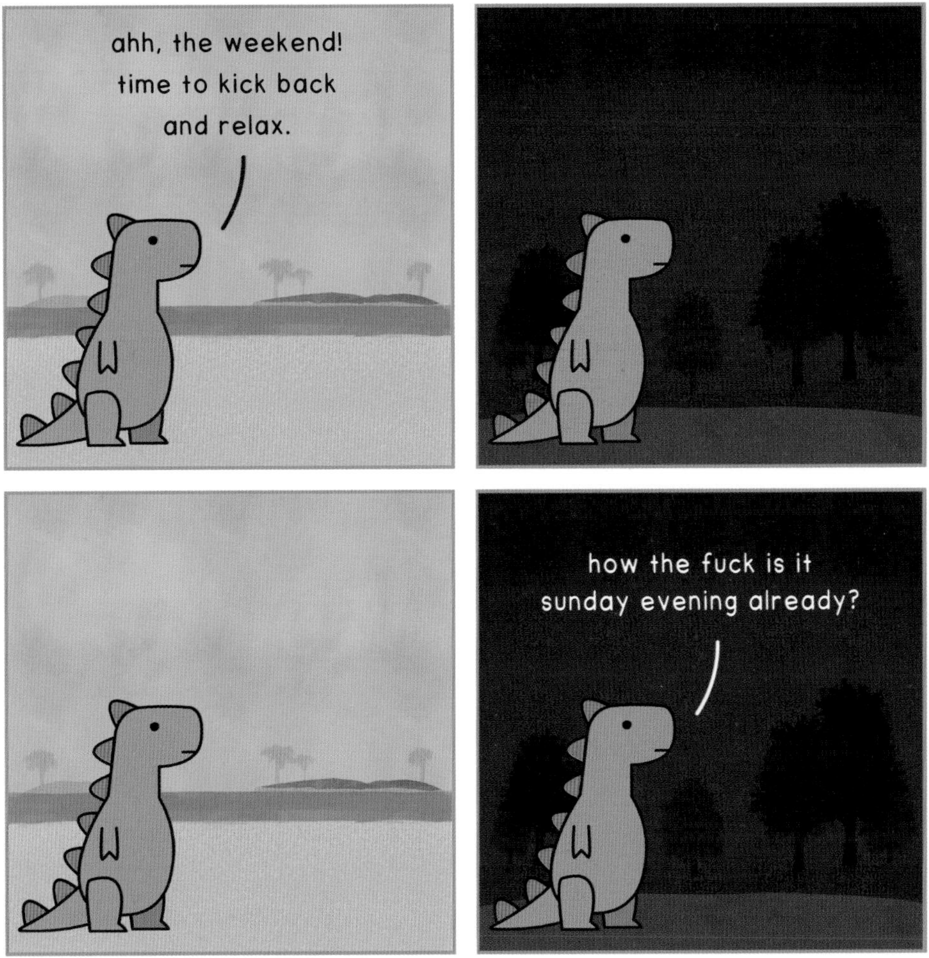
ahh, the weekend! time to kick back and relax.
how the fuck is it sunday evening already?

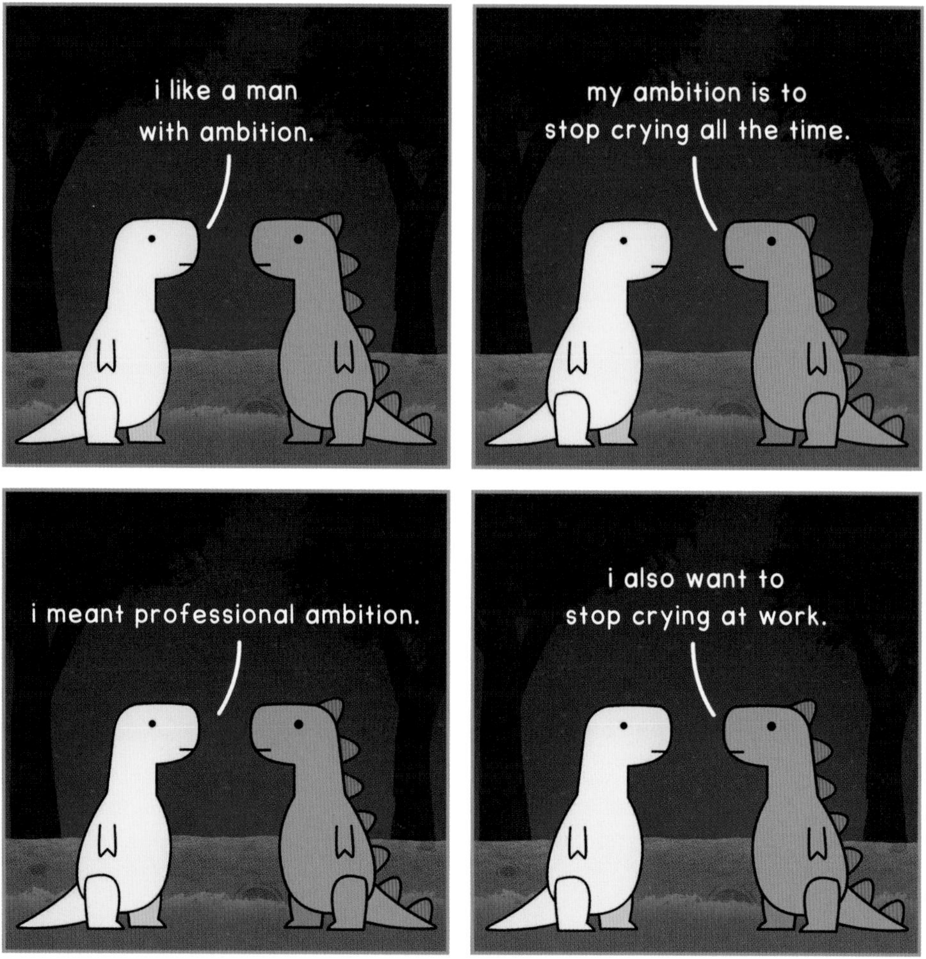
i like a man with ambition.
my ambition is to stop crying all the time.
i meant professional ambition.
i also want to stop crying at work.

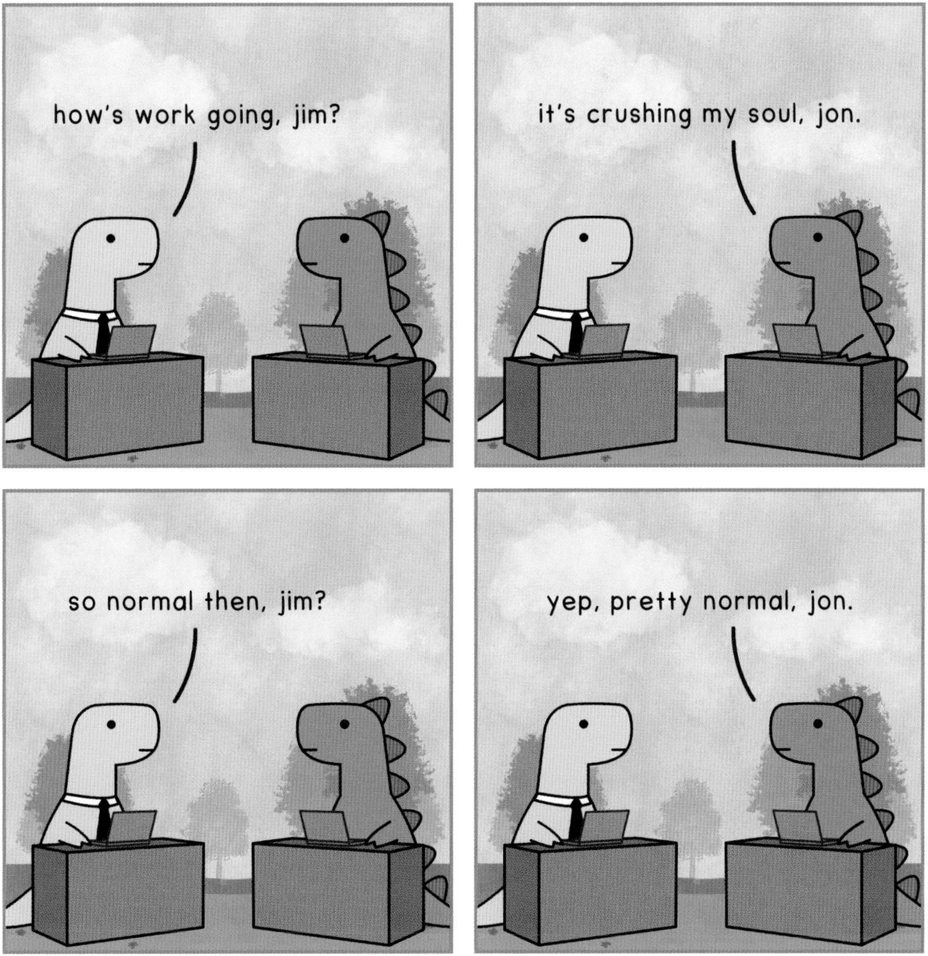
how's work going, jim?
it's crushing my soul, jon.
so normal then, jim?
yep, pretty normal, jon.

i can't concentrate on this work until i've had a break.
i can't enjoy this break until i've finished my work.

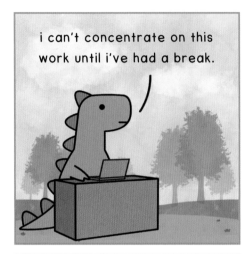

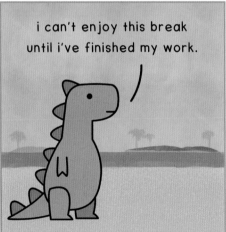

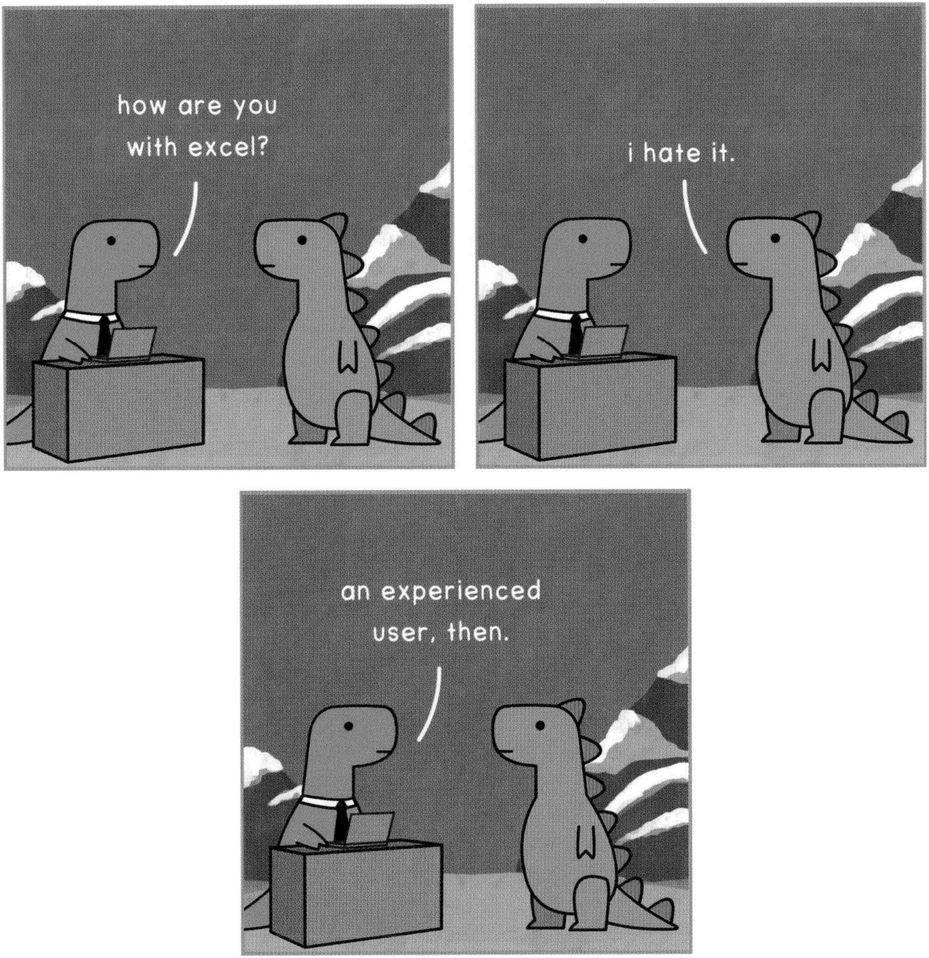
how are you with excel?
i hate it.
an experienced user, then.

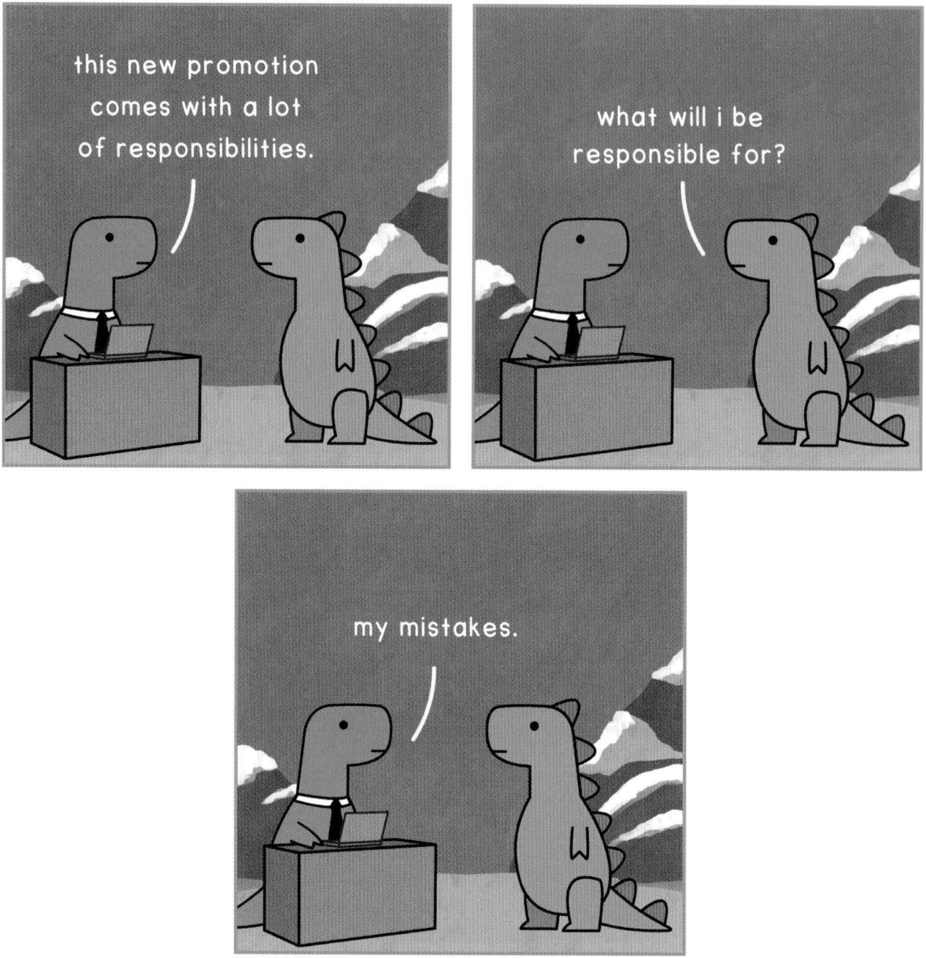
this new promotion comes with a lot of responsibilities.
what will i be responsible for?
my mistakes.

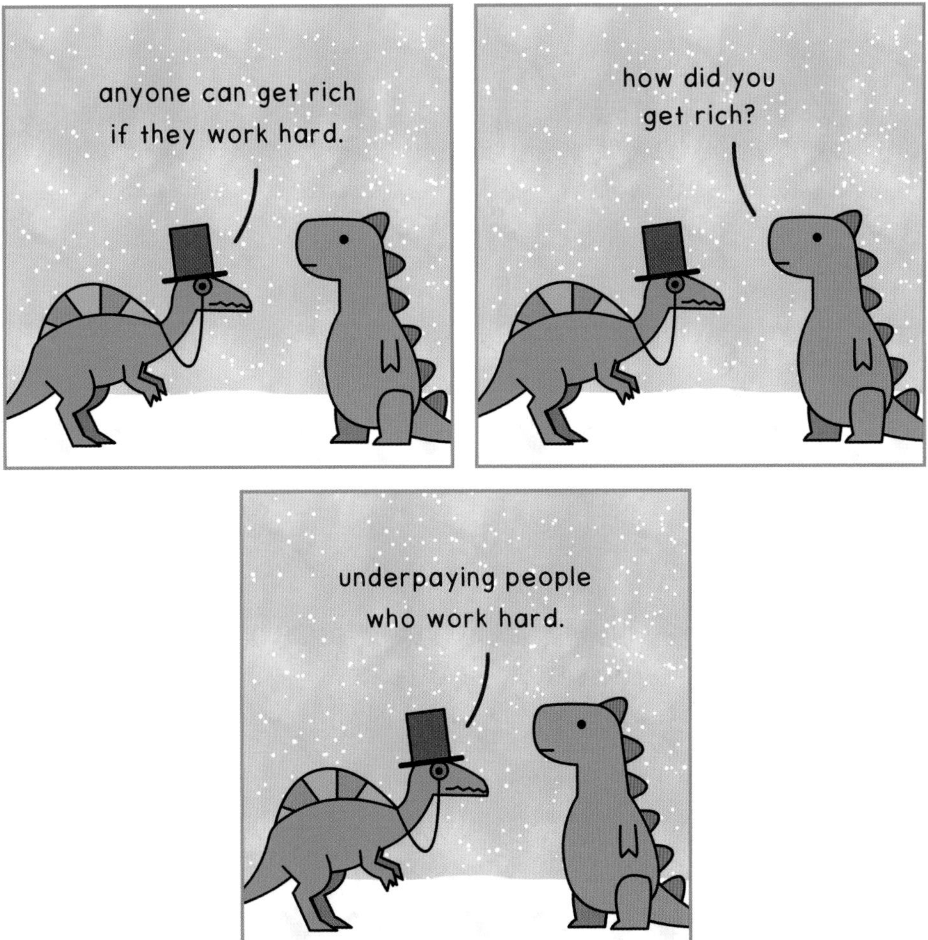
anyone can get rich if they work hard.
how did you get rich?
underpaying people who work hard.

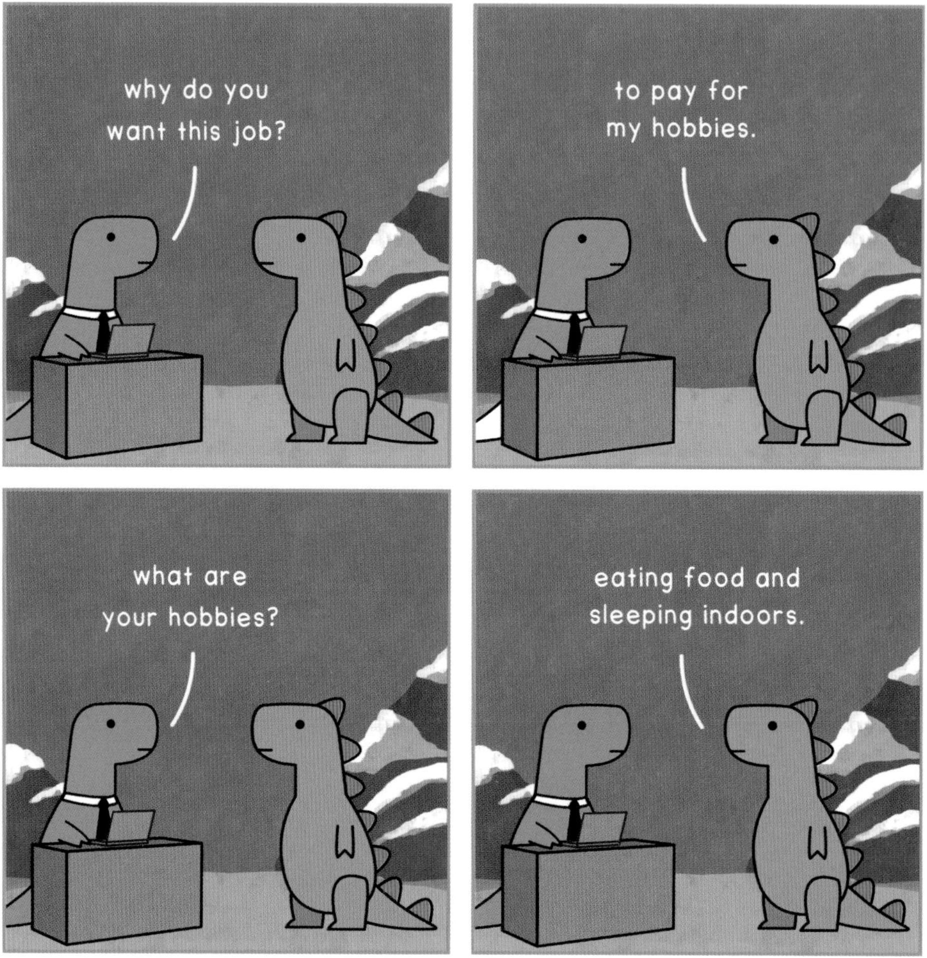
why do you want this job?
to pay for my hobbies.
what are your hobbies?
eating food and sleeping indoors.

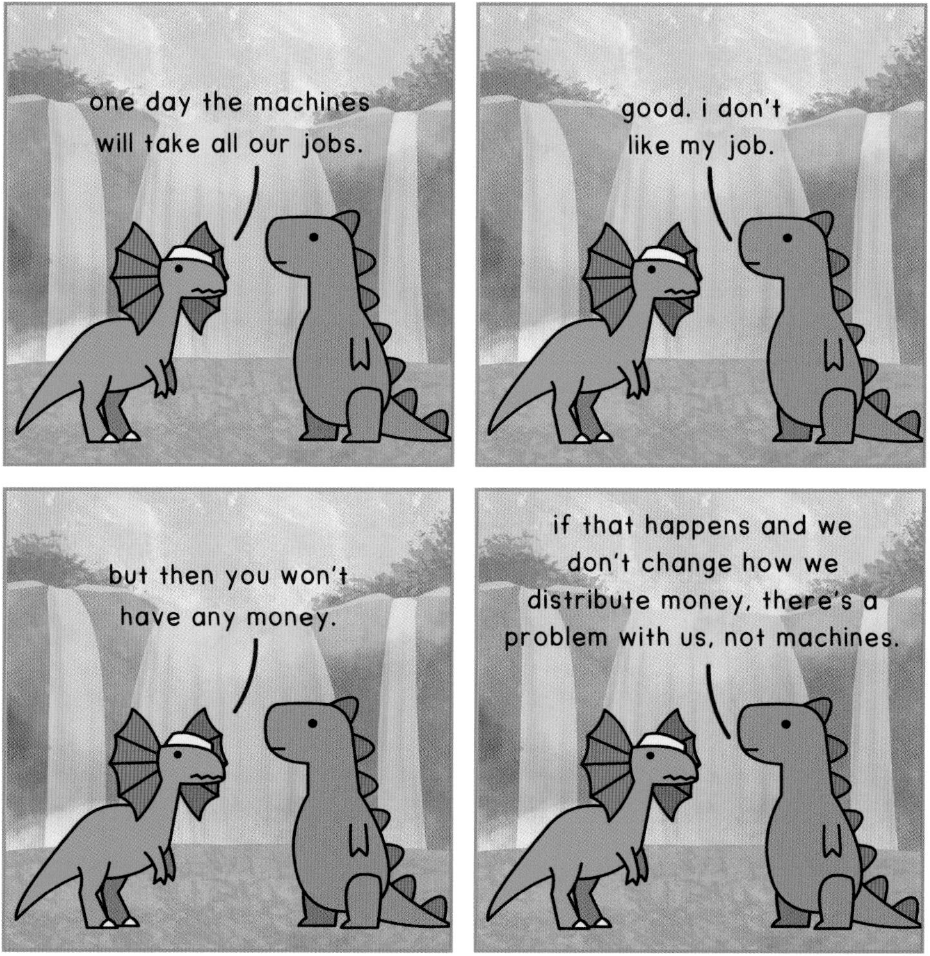
one day the machines will take all our jobs.
good. i don't like my job.
but then you won't have any money.
if that happens and we don't change how we distribute money, there's a problem with us, not machines.

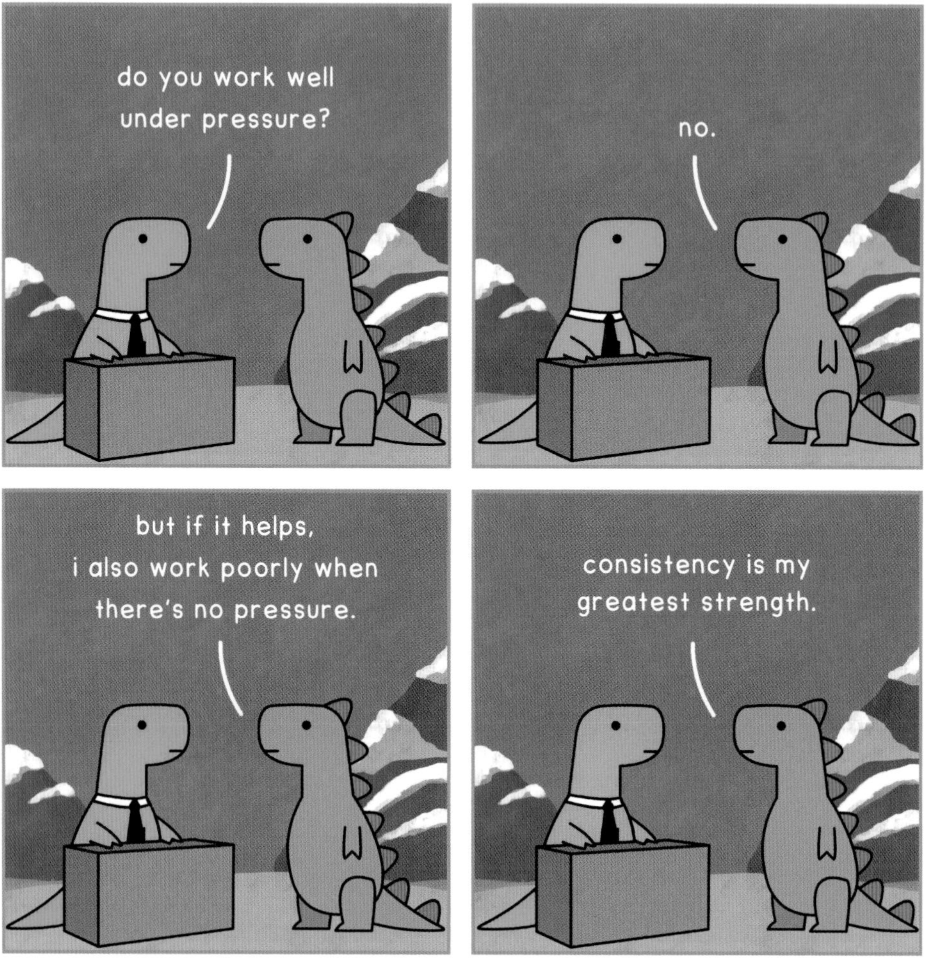
do you work well under pressure?
no.
but if it helps, i also work poorly when there's no pressure.
consistency is my greatest strength.

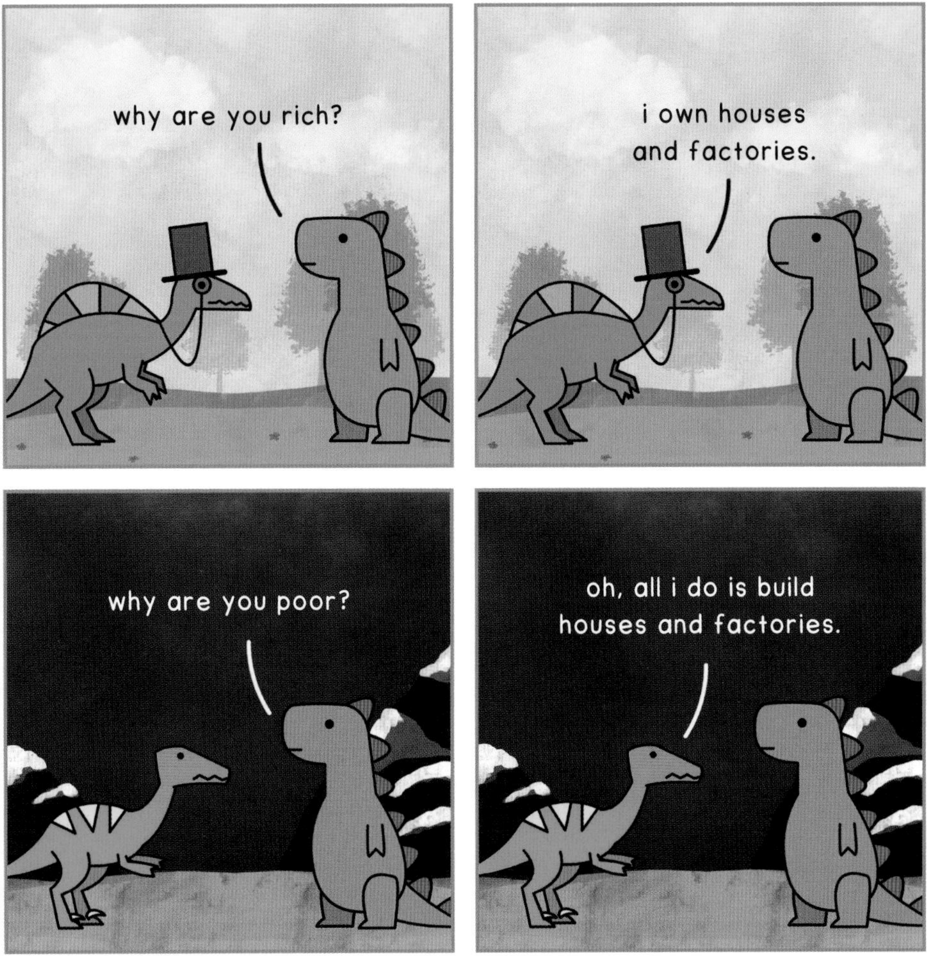
why are you rich?
i own houses and factories.
why are you poor?
oh, all i do is build houses and factories.

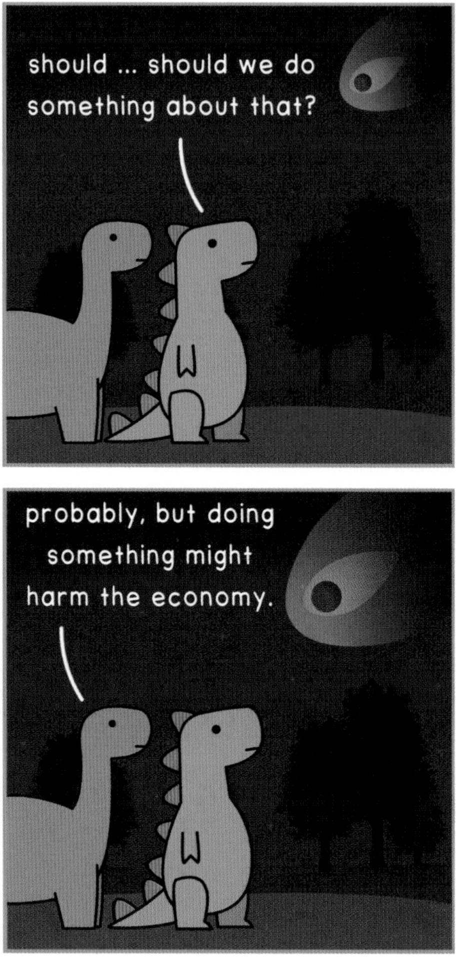
should ... should we do something about that?
probably, but doing something might harm the economy.

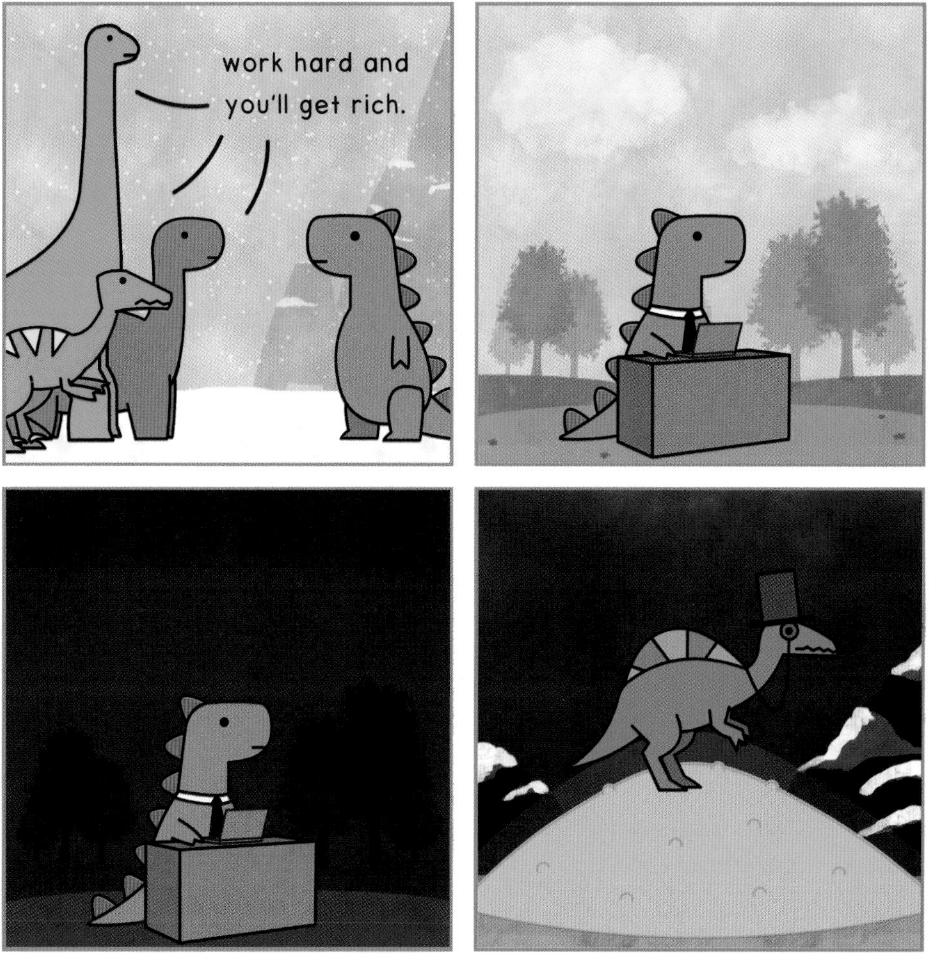
work hard and you'll get rich.

success and failure

it's the not taking part that counts

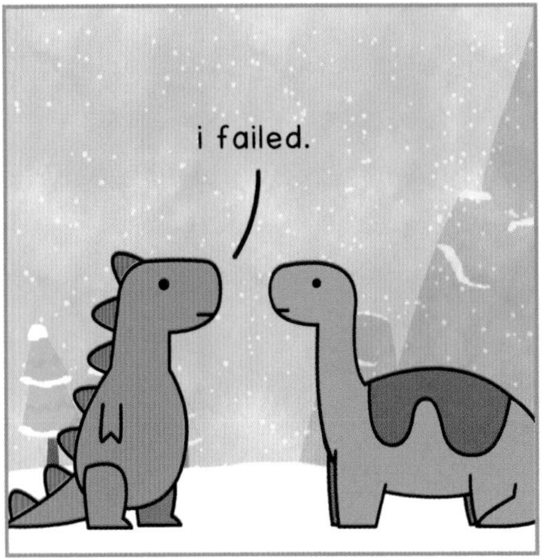
i failed.

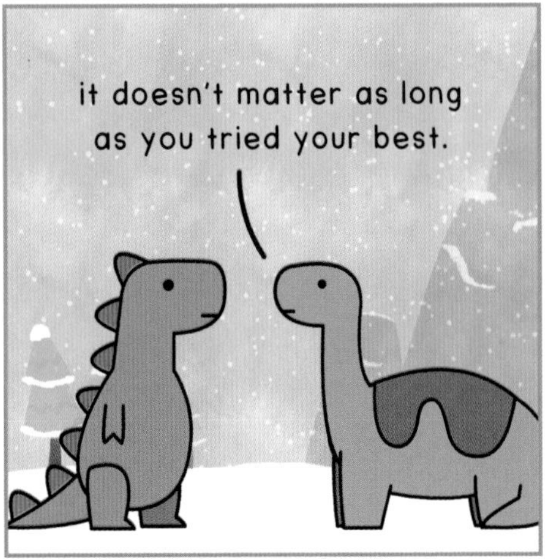
it doesn't matter as long
as you tried your best.

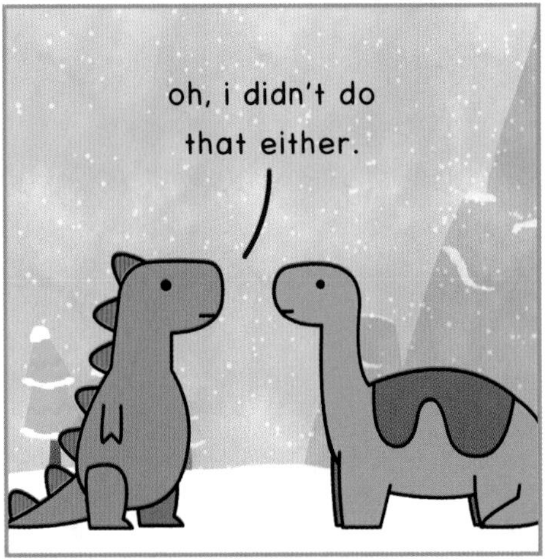
oh, i didn't do
that either.

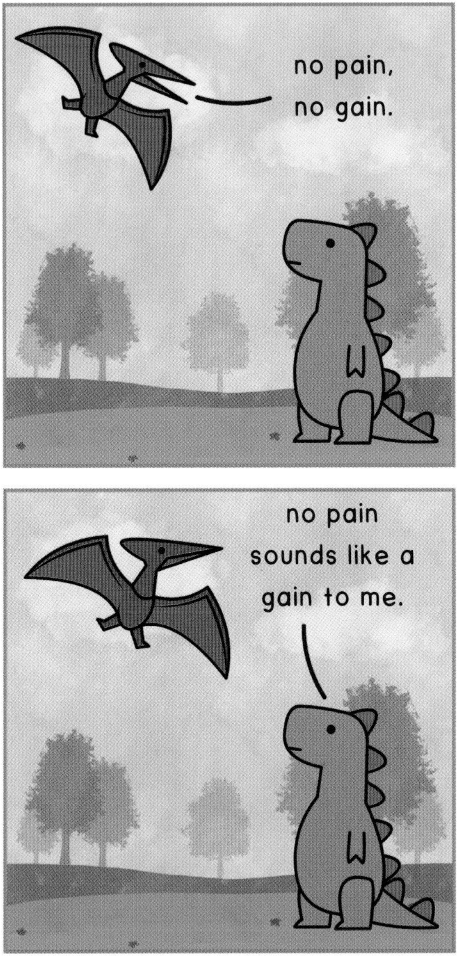
no pain,
no gain.
no pain
sounds like a
gain to me.

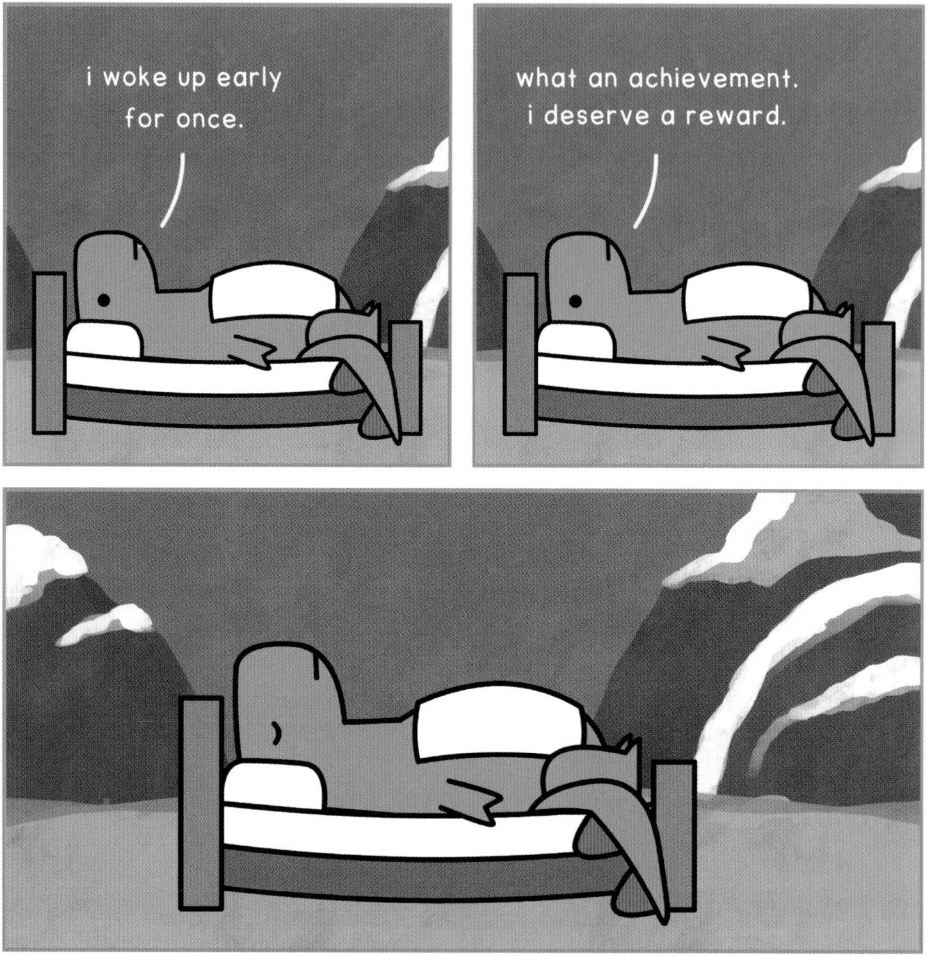
i woke up early for once.
what an achievement. i deserve a reward.

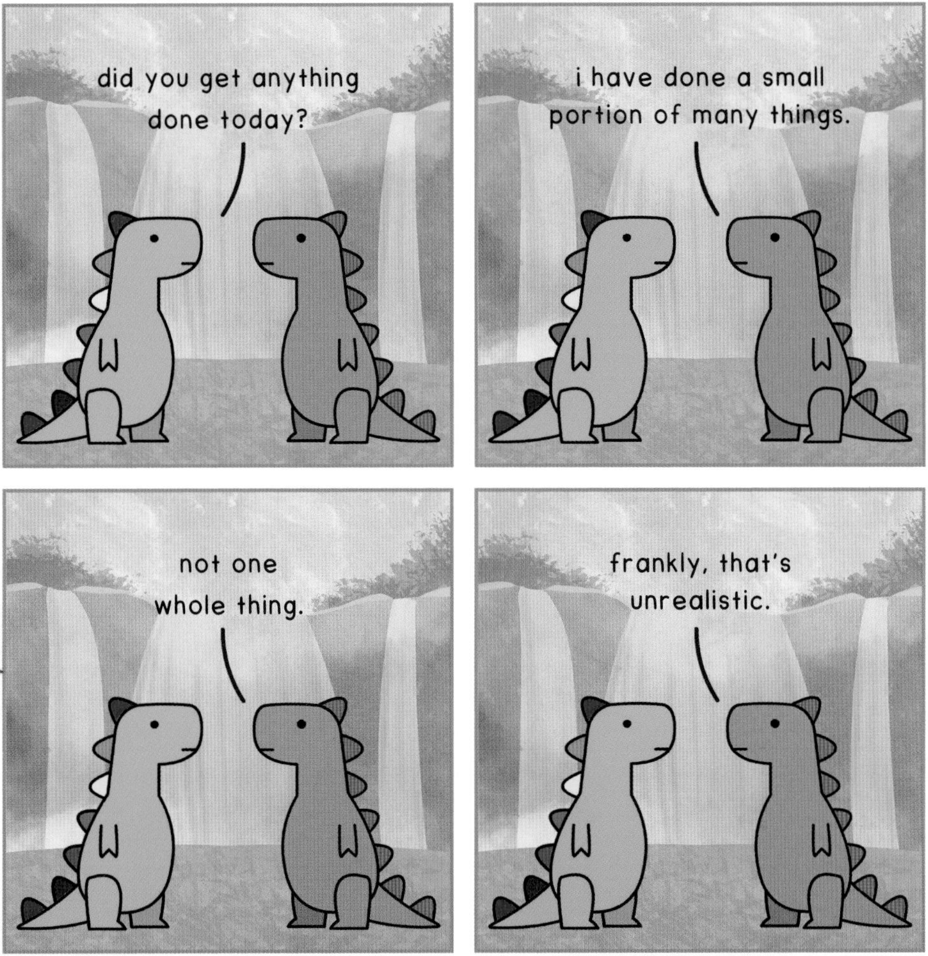
did you get anything done today?
i have done a small portion of many things.
not one whole thing.
frankly, that's unrealistic.

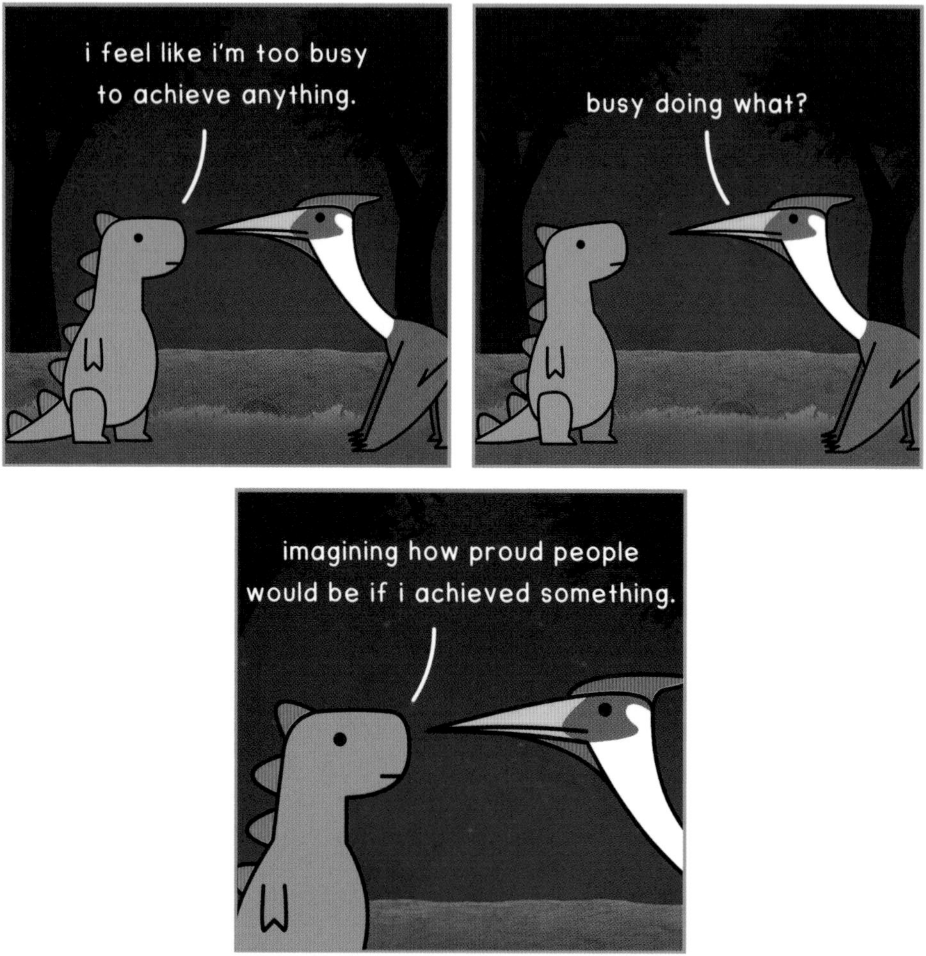
i feel like i'm too busy to achieve anything.
busy doing what?
imagining how proud people would be if i achieved something.

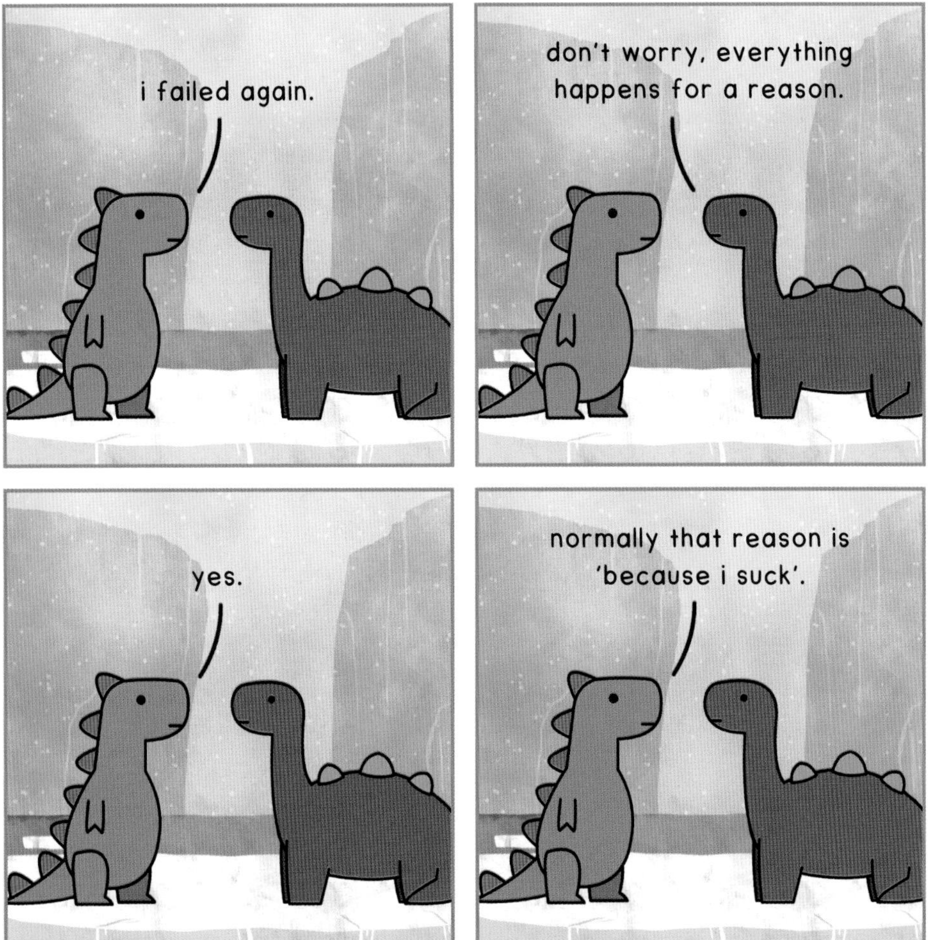
i failed again.
don't worry, everything happens for a reason.
yes.
normally that reason is 'because i suck'.

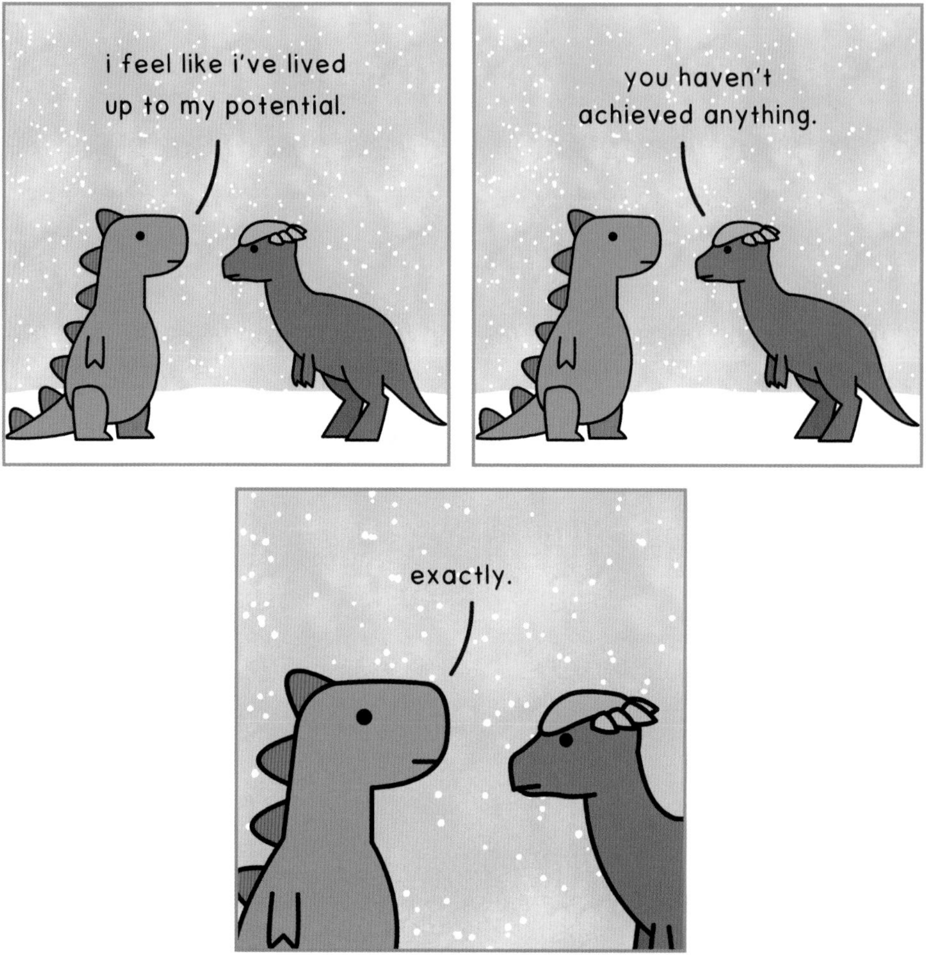
i feel like i've lived up to my potential.
you haven't achieved anything.
exactly.

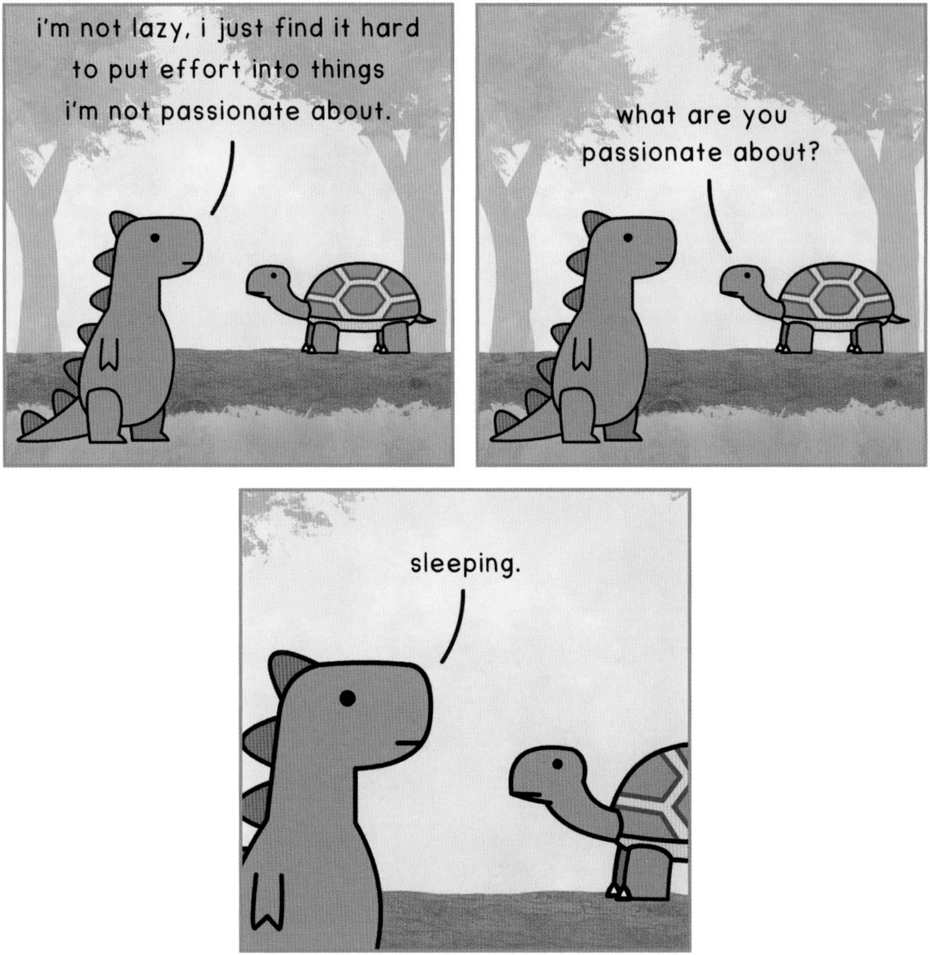
i'm not lazy, i just find it hard to put effort into things i'm not passionate about.
what are you passionate about?
sleeping.

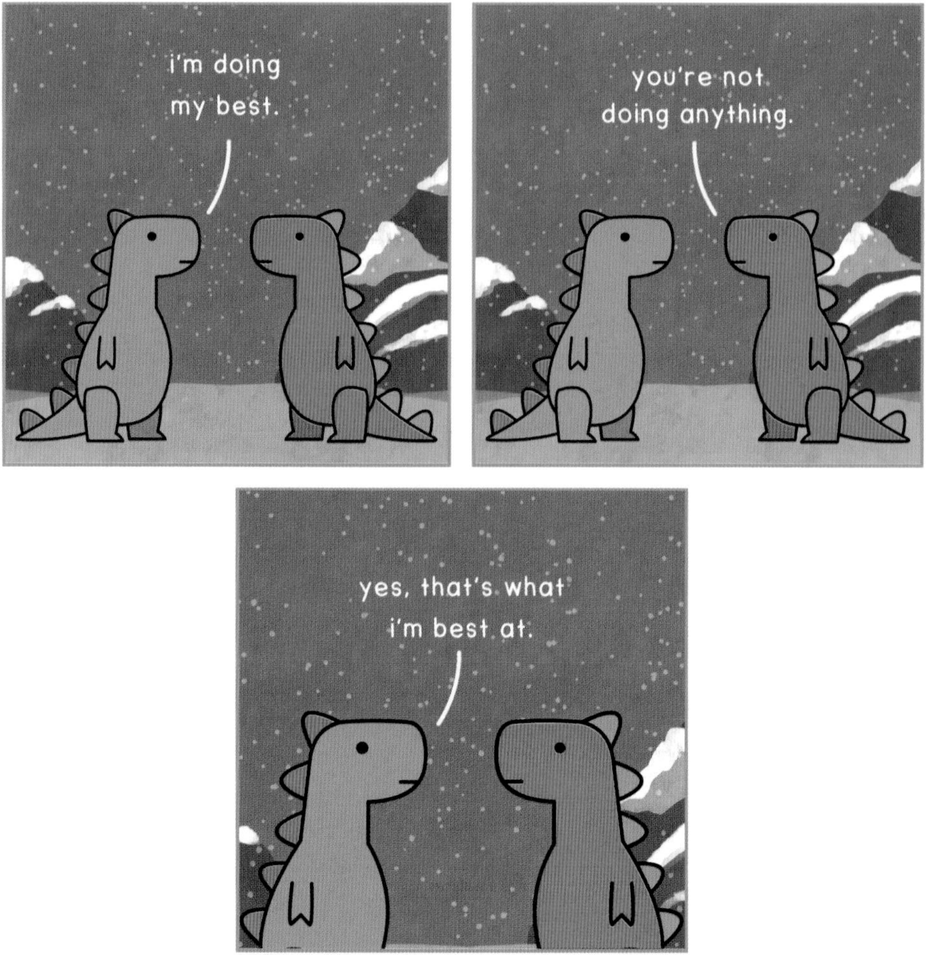
i'm doing my best.
you're not doing anything.
yes, that's what i'm best at.

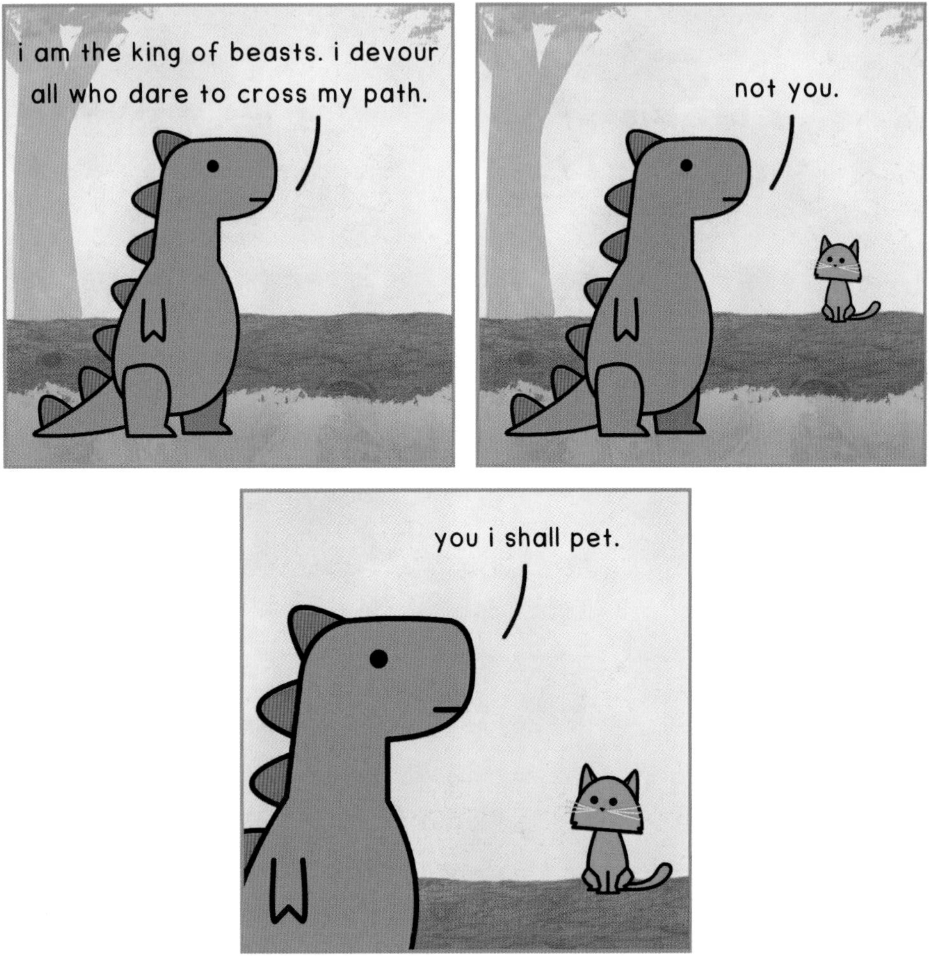
i am the king of beasts. i devour all who dare to cross my path.
not you.
you i shall pet.

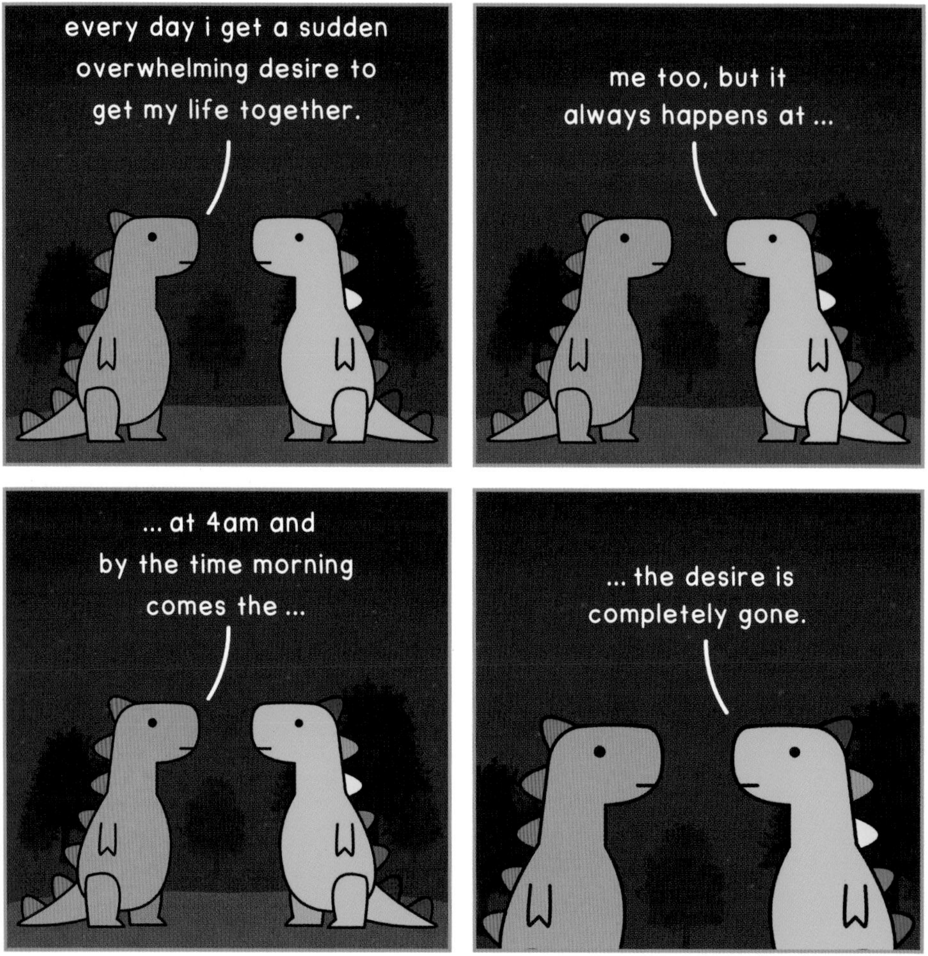
every day i get a sudden overwhelming desire to get my life together.
me too, but it always happens at ...
... at 4am and by the time morning comes the ...
... the desire is completely gone.